The Hausa language

AF577429

Languages of Asia and Africa

Languages of Asia and Africa

Volume 5
The Hausa language

A descriptive grammar

M. Smirnova

Translated by G. L. Campbell

Routledge & Kegan Paul

London, Boston, Melbourne and Henley

This translation first published in 1982
by Routledge & Kegan Paul Ltd
39 Store Street, London WC1E 7DD,
9 Park Street, Boston, Mass. 02108, USA,
296 Beaconsfield Parade, Middle Park,
Melbourne 3206, Australia and
Broadway House, Newtown Road,
Henley-on-Thames, Oxon RG9 1EN
Printed in Great Britain by
Thetford Press Ltd, Thetford, Norfolk
First published as Yazyk Hausa by
Oriental Literature Publishing House, Moscow, 1960
English translation Routledge & Kegan Paul Ltd, 1982
No part of this book may be reproduced in
any form without permission from the
publisher, except for the quotation of brief
passages in criticism

Library of Congress Cataloging in Publication Data

Smirnova, M.A. (Mirra Aleksandrovna)
The Hausa language.

(Languages of Asia and Africa, ISSN 0261-0116; v.5)
Translation of IAzyk khausa.
Bibliography: p.
1. Hausa language--Grammar. I. Title. II. Series:
Languages of Asia and Africa (Routledge & Kegan Paul);
v. 4.
PL8232.S613 493'.725 82-588
ISBN 0-7100-9076-5 AACR2

Contents

Introduction

Hausa is the language of the Hausa people, who number about 13 million. Of these, some 10 million are concentrated in Northern Nigeria; more than 1.5 million are in Niger; the remainder are found in the northern parts of Cameroun, Benin, Togo, Ghana and the Republic of Chad. Pockets of Hausa speech are also found in other West African states.

Such sources as are available for the history of West Africa have very little to say on the early history of the Hausa regions. Not until the beginning of the fifteenth century are we on firmer ground. From the fifteenth to the eighteenth centuries was the period of the great Hausa city-states, the so-called 'Hausa Seven' (Hausa bakwai): Kano, Gobir, Zanfara, Daura, Zaria, Rano, Katsina. These great trading centres lay in the territory today occupied by Northern Nigeria and Southern Niger. The Hausa traders had wide commercial connections and travelled by caravan across the Sahara to the lands of the Maghreb in North Africa. Thus, the Hausa language came to be used as a *lingua franca* throughout West Africa, in the Sudan, Morocco, Tunisia, in the Alexandria area and in Tripoli. To this day there are regions with a bilingual population, whose second language is Hausa.

In terms of the area over which it has spread, Hausa is second only to Swahili in sub-Saharan Africa, being spoken by not less than 25 million people. But as regards the number of people whose mother tongue it is, Hausa takes pride of place among the languages of Africa. It is customary to recognise three groups in Northern Nigeria speaking Hausa: true Hausas, i.e. Hausas by birth; those who have become Hausas via various processes of assimilation; a third group comprises those who use Hausa as a second, third or even fourth language. (170)

The question whether Hausa is related to any other linguistic group was for long hotly disputed, and in classifications of African languages Hausa was allotted an independent place, unconnected with any other African languages. At the same time, a solution of the problem of the genetic classification of the language was essential, not only on the purely linguistic plane but also if the question of the origins of the Hausa people was to be cleared up. (163, 165)

It can now be taken as definitively established that Hausa belongs to the Semito-Hamitic or Afro-Asiatic family of languages. (64, 31) Many features of its grammatical structure go to justify the inclusion of Hausa in this family; thus, for example, the pronominal system, certain peculiarities of conjugation and verbal formation, the presence of grammatical gender, methods of word formation and formation of the plural, separate grammatical formants. Together with certain languages spoken in the neighbourhood of Lake Chad, Hausa forms the Chadic sub-group of the Semito-Hamitic family, Hausa being the most important member of the sub-group both as regards diffusion and as regards the attention paid to it by linguists. It should be mentioned that recent years have seen a considerable advance in the number of Chadic languages studied, and the new data at our disposal have enabled us to formulate a much fuller picture of the structure of these languages as a step towards their precise classification. (154, 81)

It was in the second half of the nineteenth century that Europeans began to study Hausa. The first books on the language were those of the German missionary Schön. In 1853 he published a Hausa dictionary, (201) in 1862 a grammar (200) and in 1885 a collection of texts written down from the dictation of native speakers - Magana Hausa. The German traveller G. Barth, who spent three years in Africa, produced a dictionary of several African languages, including Hausa. (155) Apart from lists of words, this dictionary gives short grammatical sketches of each of the languages included. A few grammars and dictionaries of Hausa were produced at this time in France. (27, 122)

At the turn of the century there appeared the grammars and dictionaries of Mischlich (139, 140), Robinson (196, 197), and Delafosse. (26) All of these had a purely practical character. Scientific study of the language began with the grammars and dictionary of Abraham (1, 2, 5, 6) and the dictionary by Bargery. (14) Both Abraham and Bargery spent many years learning the language among the Hausa people in Nigeria, and their dictionaries are full of valuable lexicographical material.

In recent years, more and more scholars in many countries have turned their attention to Hausa, and some idea of the wide interest in the language may be gained from the extensive bibliography appended to the present work. In conclusion, it is worth while making special mention of the Hausa grammar published in 1953 in England by A. Howeidy. (83) It serves purely practical ends and contains nothing new - but it is the first grammar of Hausa written by a Hausa.

Before the Europeans arrived in the Hausa lands, Hausa already possessed an indigenous system of writing based on the Arabic script, called Ajami. Texts written in Ajami are for the most part historical chronicles, legends and folk-tales. When Nigeria became an English colony, a system of writing based on the English alphabet was devised for Hausa. In this system, (the so-called 'Coko'), certain sounds proper to Hausa are indicated by modified letters, e.g. ɓ, ɗ, ƙ. Digraphs are also used: sh = š, ts = c.

The Hausa alphabet: a, b, ɓ, c, d, ɗ, e, f, g, h, i, j, k, ƙ, l, m, n, o, p, r, s, t, u, w, y, 'y, z.

The 'glottal stop' (see 'Phonetics') in alphabetisation is disregarded, but all vowel-initial words are pronounced with a glottal stop. Words beginning with sh and ts are placed in the dictionary under s and t correspondingly.

There are translations into Hausa of the Bible and various other texts of a religious nature. Europeans have published much folklore material (folk-tales, legends, poems) reflecting different dialects of Hausa.

Dialects: there are several dialects, of which the two most important are the Kano dialect (Eastern) and the Sokoto dialect (Western). Differences between the Hausa dialects are primarily of a phonetic nature.* However, there are also lexical and morphological differences: for example, in the forms and uses of certain pronouns; in the Kano dialect the feminine participle has the ending -iya, plural -u, but the Sokoto dialect has -a for the former ending and -i for the latter, etc. Neither phonetic differences nor

* Some phonological peculiarities of these dialects are mentioned in the section on Phonetics (p. 6).

morphological discrepancies, however, prevent speakers of the various Hausa dialects from understanding each other. At present, a literary form of Hausa based on the Kano dialect is taking shape, and work is proceeding on unifying the orthography. (32, 67) Much work has been done by the Hausa Language Board, set up in 1955 to further the standardisation of written Hausa. (95) Northern Nigeria has Hausa newspapers and educational textbooks; local authors have their works printed in Hausa and there are also translations from European languages. Early in the 1930s, the 'Hausa Translation Bureau' was established in Zaria. In 1954 this was renamed NORLA (Northern Region Literature Agency); it is now called the Gaskiya Corporation. This agency publishes all sorts of material in Hausa. Radio broadcasts in Hausa are carried on both by local and by foreign stations. Hausa is recognised together with English as the official language of administration and politics in Northern Nigeria. (170, 241)

Chapter 1

Phonetics

The basic vowels of Hausa may be set out diagramatically as follows: non-labialised vowels appear to the right of the line in each row, the labialised sounds to the left: the sounds are ranged from top to bottom in order of grade:

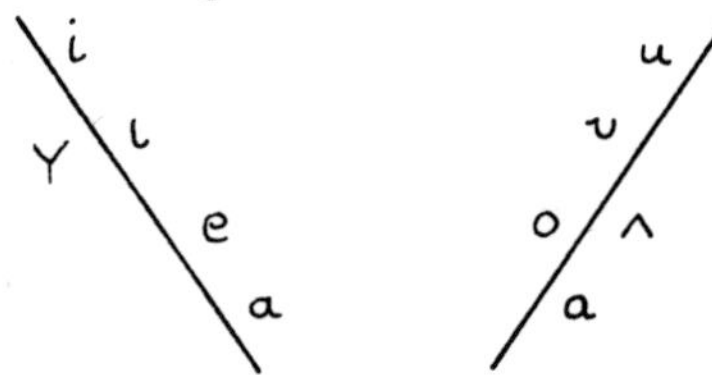

All vowel sounds may be either long or short. Length is indicated only in texts written in Ajami; the contemporary script does not indicate length.

Hausa has four diphthongs: /aɩ/, /eɩ/, /ɔɩ/ and /au/. In the script, the three former are realised as ai, the fourth as au.

/ei/ is pronounced in the words sai = but and kai = you (but /kaɩ/ = head) and a few others:

ai is pronounced as /ɔɩ/ when preceded by w: karuwai = thieves, kwai = egg.

* The treatment of Hausa phonetics here presented is based on the descriptions given by Bargery, Abraham, Klingenheben, Taylor, Yushmanov, Greenberg and a few others.

In most cases, ai sounds as /ai/.

The diphthong /au/ is labialised. All Hausa diphthongs are falling.

Sometimes diphthongs show a tendency to contract into long monophthongs. It is difficult to say what causes this phenomenon. Both forms - the diphthong and the contraction - exist alongside each other:

daina and dēna = to despise

kau and kō = and, also

A principal characteristic of the Hausa consonantal system is the presence of the glottal stop both independently and in combination with certain consonants. The presence of palatalised and labialised back consonants (post-dorsals) should also be noticed. In the script, the labialisation of a consonant is indicated by putting w after it, while postposition of y indicates palatalisation.

Table 1 sets out the basic consonantal sounds of Hausa. Positional variants and dialectal peculiarities are not shown; the most important of these are shown below. In each square of the table, the sounds are arranged from left to right in the following order: surd without glottal stop, voiced without glottal stop, surd with glottal stop and voiced with glottal stop.

Unoccupied positions are indicated by a dash.

The sounds /b/, /č/ and /dʒ/ (in the script c and j), /t/ and /d/, /s/ and /z/, /š/ (in the script sh), /k/ and /g/, /h/, /l/, /m/, /n/, /ŋ/, /j/ (in the script y) are very much like the equivalent English sounds.

The bilabial (obstruent) /p/ is also articulated very like the English p but the accompanying aspiration is stronger. The sound /p/ is found only in the Kano dialect, and even in this dialect many speakers pronounce it as /f/.

Table 1 The Hausa consonants

	Place of articulation / Method of articulation	Bilabial	Pre-dental	Dorsal	Post-dorsal			Glottal
					Palatalised	Simple	Labialised	
Plosives	Pure	p b - ɓ	t d - ɗ		k' g' k' -	k g k -	k° g° k° -	ʔ - - -
	Affricate		č dʒ c -					
	Sonant	-m- -	-n - -			- ŋ - -		
Fricatives	Unvoiced	f-	s z - - š					h - - -
	Voiced	- w - -	l	j - - -				
Rolled	Single flap		- ɍ - -					
	Trilled		- r - -					

In the Western dialects /f/ or /h/ correspond to Eastern Hausa /p/; /f/ and /h/ are freely interchangeable in Hausa in any position. In the Katsina dialect, in addition to the bilabial /f/ there is also a labio-dental /f/.

Both the postdorsal sonant /ŋ/ and the predental /n/ are represented in the script by the letter n. The sound /ŋ/ is found medially before /g,k,w/ and finally if the next word begins with the glottal stop or with /h/. In many borrowings from Arabic and in certain adverbs and conjunctions (e.g. nan = here; can = there; kadan = if) final /n/ is preserved irrespective of the initial sound in the following word.

In the same way, the two variants of r: /r/ and /ɽ/ are not distinguished in script although they have phonemic status: (cf. 152, 69)

/bara/ = request for alms, and /baɽa/ = servant.

/r/ is rolled while /ɽ/ is a single-flap sound intermediate between /r/ and /l/; it is pronounced by bringing the tip of the tongue up and bending it backwards further than in the case of /l/ and /r/. To the single-flap /ɽ/ of the Kano dialect there often corresponds in other dialects /l/.*

The glottal stop /ʔ/ (represented in the script by the apostrophe) is formed by contraction and subsequent rapid release of the vocal chords. This glottal sound occurs independently (e.g. in Arabic) and also contributes to the formation of particular sounds. One such sound is the post-dorsal obstruent /ƙ/ which differs from ordinary /k/ in the presence of the glottal stop. It has no voiced variant. /k/ like the other post-dorsals /g/ and /k/ can be labialised and palatalised.

* The sign ɽ to represent the single-flap r is taken from (14).

The front affricate /c/ (written as ts) is apical and accompanied by the glottal stop.* It has no voiced variant.

/ɓ/ and /ɗ/ differ from ordinary /b/ and /d/ in that they are accompanied by the glottal stop, and, in addition, are inspiratory rather than expiratory, that is to say, they are implosives.

The basic law affecting sounds in the flow of Hausa speech is that of repressive assimilation, either total or partial. Partial assimilation can be seen in consonantal shift before front vowels. As a rule, this sound change takes place in the final syllable of a word and in certain morphological conditions:

t > c: ɓata = to squander - ɓace (same meaning, before a grammatical object);

d > j: gwada = to measure - gwaje or gwaji (same meaning before grammatical object);

s > sh: rasa = to be short of something - rashi = insufficiency;

hausa = Hausa - bahaushe = Hausa person;

z > j: kaza = hen - kaji = hens.

Occasionally, the non-palatalised consonants t, d, s, z are retained before e and i in a final syllable; this is particularly frequent in borrowings:

asibiti = hospital (< English)

taksi = taxi (< English)

gadi = guard (< English)

Before the bilabials b, f, m, final n > m. This shift is a variant of full assimilation: abin mamaki > abim mamaki = something astonishing. Final r is totally assimilated to following t or s:

* According to some authorities, /c/ is accompanied by strong tension of the articulatory organs, not by the glottal stop.

rigar sarki > rigas sarki = the chief's clothes.

Full assimilation of this type is always indicated in the Ajami script and sometimes even in the Latin alphabet.

Total assimilation of consonants is frequent in the formation of the intensive form of the verb which involves reduplication of the root:

buga = to beat, bubbuga = to beat mercilessly (not *bubbuga)

kama = catch, kakkama = catch a lot of (not *kamkama)

also in some borrowed words, e.g.

littafi = book (< Maghrebi Arabic/ ləkta:b/)

likkafa = stirrup (< Maghrebi Arabic/lərka:b/)

Complete regressive assimilation of a vowel takes place when the directional particle ma precedes a pronoun: in these circumstances, the vowel of the particle is completely assimilated to the vowel of the pronoun: thus,

ma + su > musu = to them; ma + ni > mini = to me, etc.

Structurally the syllable in Hausa is very precisely defined. The main rule is that there can be no accumulation of consonants within the confines of one syllable. If two consonants come together in a word, they are obligatorily separated into two different syllables:

kar-ba = to receive

kus-ku-re = mistake, blunder.

This requirement goes to explain the presence of additional vowels in borrowed words, e.g.:

direba = driver (< English),

firamare = primary school (< English 'primary')

suwaita = sweater (< English).

Additional vowels are also added to Hausa words ending on a consonant, when they have to take the suffix -n:

mutum = man + -n > mutumin (not *mutumn)

malam = teacher, literate + -n > malamin (not *malamn)

Hausa has two types of syllable - open and closed. The vowel of an open syllable may be either short or long, and either pure or diphthong:

da-fa = to boil, cook

fā-ra = to begin

sau-ra = residue.

The vowel in a closed syllable is always short and pure:

lar-di = district

san-da = stick, staff.

When an open syllable with a long vowel is closed, by addition of an ending, the vowel loses its length:

bakī = mouth - bakin duniya = public opinion.

A diphthong in similar circumstances loses its second element:

rai + -n > ran (not *rain)

malamai + -n > malaman (not *malamain).

The syllable always begins with a consonant. Words which the script shows as beginning with a vowel have, in fact, a glottal stop as initial.*

Only a few consonants are allowed to stand in final position in a closed syllable. These are primarily the sonants n, ŋ, m, l, r, and, much less frequently, the pre-dentals s and z, and the bilabials b and f (or p). t and k are found as finals in closed syllables in words of interjectional or adverbial nature:

fat, ƙat = completely

tak = perfectly, absolutely

birjik = in plenty

The sound k is found at the end of a few borrowings:

tak-si = taxi (< English)

da-rek-ta = director (< English).

* The script does not indicate /ʔ/ in initial position.

The letter h at the end of Allah is notated in the script but is not pronounced.

As a rule the last syllable of a word is open. Hence, closed final syllables in borrowed words customarily receive an additional vowel:

adireshi = address (< English)
kati = ticket (< English 'card')
lodi = weight, load (< English 'load)
jahili = ignorance (< Arabic /jahil/)
alkalami = pen (< Arabic /alqalam/).

A few verbal forms have a final closed syllable, e.g.:

sayas = to sell

and so do a group of words consisting mainly of adverbs:

abadan = for ever
kaf = completely

conjunctions:

kadan = if

prepositions:

cikin = in

interjections and onomatopoeic words:

ɓam = onomatopoeic word used when opening a bottle.

Many borrowed words also retain a closed syllable as final:

nas = nurse (< English 'nurse')
fayaman = fireman (< English 'fireman')
afil = appeal (< English 'appeal).

In the construct state, nouns acquire a final closed syllable

baki = bank - bakin kogi = the bank of the river.

In some cases, the syllable consists of a single consonant (n or m): ...n zo = in order that I should come; ...m ba = in order that I should give.

There was for long no agreement among scholars as to whether Hausa is or is not a tonal language. German students of the language maintained that it was not, and sought to account for its phonology in terms of tonic stress. English and American authorities on the other hand treated Hausa as a tonal language and postulated a connection between tone and stress. In the Preface to his dictionary, Bargery writes that the role of tone is not so significant in Hausa as it is in such undoubtedly tonal languages as Yoruba for example. At the same time, tone in Hausa is on occasion phonemic in that it alone distinguishes homographs, thus:

busa̱ = to blow, bu̥sa = to winnow grain and bu̱sa = a piece of boiled potato

fasa̱ = to destroy, fḁsa̱ = destruction.*

In other words, tone in Hausa differentiates both form and significance.

Nor are the authorities agreed as to the exact number of tones in Hausa. According to Bargery, there are six: high and high falling, middle and middle falling, low and low falling. Greenberg distinguishes three: high, low and mixed; Abraham has only two: high and low. The falling tones represent transitional stages between one basic tone and another. Tone is not reflected in Hausa orthography. It is only in basic dictionaries of the language and in works devoted specifically to the problems of tone in Hausa that tone marks are given.

Stress in Hausa is free, that is, it is associated with no one fixed position in the word. Taken in isolation, every Hausa word has a specific stress which usually falls on the penultimate syllable. In conjunction with other words how-

* The examples are taken from (14). A line below the vowel indicates low tone, a circle indicates middle; where there is no subscript, the tone is high.

ever, or when a given word is modulated by prefixes and suffixes, the stress pattern may change.

Certain regularities in stress pattern associated with specific forms of words may be noticed. Thus, the nominal plural suffixes -ái and -úna are always stressed:

dogarái = policemen

sandúna = sticks

the verbal ending -o indicating that the action is directed towards the speaker:

tafó = to come

and the nominal prefix má-

máƙeri = blacksmith

are also invariably stressed. The possessive and objective pronouns affect the position of the stress which shifts to the syllable preceding these pronouns:

ríga = clothes - rigársa = his clothes

ina dúba = I look - ina dubánsa = I look at him.

Chapter 2

Vocabulary and word-formation

The major part of the Hausa vocabulary consists of native Hausa words, both simple and derived. Simple nouns and verbs are polysemantic to a high degree. Here, for example, are some meanings of the word kara:

(1) stem, stalk

(2) a measure of length

(3) a needle for making nets

(4) a spacer in script.

The verb raba has the following meanings:

(1) divide, to distribute

(2) to abolish

(3) to halt, suspend.

Certain verbs of perception have particularly many meanings: thus ji means not only 'to hear', but also 'to understand', 'to feel', 'to smell', 'to listen to', 'to worry', 'to be troubled about something'; ci means not only 'to eat' but also 'to win, gain', 'to conquer', 'to win a contest'.

With the exception of the adjectives denoting colours, words indicating qualities and many adverbs have as a rule a large number of synonyms. Certain restrictions operate however in the choice and use of these synonyms. For example, the word babba = big can be used of any object, any human being or animal, but other words also meaning 'big' such as bangwali, dakwal-dakwal, kwadali, tulu-tulu, etc. can only be used of something round in shape; ingarma, kisagare, shimgege, etc. can only be applied to human beings and animals; birkeke, wangameme, wangami can only be used of territory, spatial extension. The adverb ƙwarai = very is used to indicate an intensification of any quality or action; but ƙirin with the same meaning is only used of something dark in shade:

baƙi ƙirin = very black

duhu ƙirin = extraordinary darkness, i.e. very dark.

There are certain adverbs meaning 'very' which are used invariably in connection with specific words:

ja = red - ja wur = dark red or bright red (very red)

kore = green - kore shar = dark green (very green).

Hausa has a large number of stable compounds which vary greatly in make-up. For example, two nouns may be used together in the construct state, marked by -n final of the first component:

kaya = weight, load + aiki = work > kayan aiki = equipment required for work

kaya = weight, load + doki = horse > kayan doki = horse-cloth

rashi = absence of something + kunya = shame > rashin kunya = shamelessness

jirgi = boat + sama = sky > jirgin sama = aircraft

ƙwallo = ball + tebur = table > ƙwallon tebur = table tennis.

The prefix mai- indicating possession of something is sometimes added to compounds of this type:

bakin ƙai = ignorance - mai-baƙin kai = ignorant man (literally 'he who possesses a benighted head) mai- may also serve to connect two nouns, thus forming a compound of the type:

tauraro mai-wutsiya = comet (literally 'star - owner of a tail').

Verbs may also form part of compounds. For example, in the compound ba-kukan hantsi (the name of a poisonous snake: literally, 'the one which causes a cry in the morning') ba is a verb, meaning 'to cause, to provoke'. There are more complex compounds into whose composition not only nouns and verbs but also pronouns and prepositions enter:

je ka da gammo = help which people give each other by carrying grain from the fields to the houses: literally, 'go with a cushion' (gammo = cushion placed on the head when carrying a load).

Compounds containing a verb sometimes take prefixes, e.g. mai:

ba da labari = to give news - mai ba da labari - correspondent: literally, 'he who gives news'

and abin:

abin ƙara murya = microphone: literally, 'that which strengthens the voice'.

Word formation in Hausa proceeds mainly by affixation. The affixes used for this purpose range from such unproductive or completely sterile affixes as -ko and -ya which are retained in a small number of words, to highly productive ones which are now playing a very active part in the formation of new lexical items, e.g. mai-, ma-, etc.

Substantives with concrete meaning are formed from nouns and verbs with the help of prefixes and suffixes. The most important are:

mai (added to nouns):

mai- + hankali = mind > mai-hankali = clever man

mai- + gona = field > mai-gona = owner of a field.

Nouns with this prefix formed from abstract nouns are also used as adjectives:

mai-hankali = clever man and clever (< hankali = intelligence, sense)

mai-kyau = handsome man and handsome (< kyau = beauty)

maras- added to nouns indicates the negative:

maras- + hankali > maras-hankali = stupid, unintelligent

maras- + amfani = use > maras-amfani = useless (man, object).

ba- in combination with the suffix -e forms a noun defining a person in terms of his ethnic or geographical origins; it is added to the nominal base:

bahaushe = Hausa person (from hausa)

bakane = inhabitant of Kano (from Kano).

Sometimes this prefix is used to designate the profession, duty or description of a man in terms of a particular quality or peculiarity of his:

bafada/bafade = courtier (< fada = court)

bahago = left-handed person (< hagu = left side).

ma- (added to verbs):

ma'aikata = factory (as place of work; from aikata = to work)

maƙera = forge, smithy (from ƙera = to forge).

Combination of the prefix ma- with the suffix -i forms names of occupations or professions, and also place or means of work:

makoyi = teacher (from koya = to teach)

madafi = kitchen (from dafa = to boil, cook)

maɗauki = handle, shaft (from ɗauka = to take).

The suffix -ci is used to form the names of languages:

turanci = English

larabci = Arabic.

The suffixes -ya and -au (added to verbs) do not produce very many words:

kaya = load, weight (from kai = to carry)

mantau = forgetful man (from manta = to forget)

biyau = child following its mother (from biya = to follow).

Certain words which are used in the formation of concrete substantives have almost become prefixes but have not yet lost their own original meanings: thus, ɗa = son and abu = thing. Compounds containing these words are then formally two nouns in the construct state (i.e. ɗa > ɗan, abu > abin):

ɗan kunce = fighter (from kunce = fight)

ɗan kujera = deputy, representative (from kujera = chair)

abin mamaki = something wonderful (from mamaki = wonder)

abin tsoro = something frightful (from tsoro = fear)

In the word abinci = food (literally, thing to eat) abin has lost all association with its original meaning.

The formation of abstracta from nominal bases takes place by means of the suffixes -ci (-nci), -ta (-nta), -taka (-ntaka):

bahili = miserly - bahilci = greed

ango = suitor - angwanci = engagement

bawa = slave - bauta = slavery

samari = youth (person) - samartaka = youthful ways

mugu = bad - mugunta = evil.

Abstract nouns are formed from verbs with the help of the suffixes -wa, -ayya, -eniyya, -au, and also from the relatively unproductive suffix -ko

dubawa = looking (from duba = to look at)

soyayya = mutual love (from so = to love)

aikatau = work for pay (from aikata = to work)

taiko = help (from taya = to help)

The prefix ma- plus the suffix -i added to a verb form abstract nouns of the type mafari = beginning (from fara = to begin).

Feminine nouns denoting female beings are formed from masculine nouns denoting male beings by means of the suffixes -a, -uwa, -iya, -wa, -nya, -niya, thus:

kafiri = infidel - kafira = female infidel

tsofo = old man - tsofuwa = old woman

kane = younger brother - kanwa = younger sister

yaro = boy - yarinya = girl

makafo = blind man - makauniya = blind woman

Not all nouns denoting female beings, however, are thus formed from masculine nouns; there are also suppletive pairings:

uba = father - uwa = mother

miji = man - mace = woman

the same goes for animals:

doki = horse - godiya = mare

zakara = cock - kaza = hen

muzuru = tomcat - kyanwa = she-cat, etc.

In addition to the prefix mai-, which we have already mentioned, there are several other ways of forming adjectives. They can be formed from abstract nouns by reduplicating the root and changing the ending:

fadi = width - faffada = wide

gautsi = fragility - gaggautsa = fragile

One series of adjectives is formed by the addition of the prefix na- for the masculine gender and ta- for the feminine:

nagari = fine (masculine), tagari = fine (feminine).

The ordinals are formed in the same way:

na-biyu = second (from biyu = two), ta-biyu (feminine) etc. The word for 'first' is formed in the same way but not from the number ɗaya = one but from the word fari = beginning: na-fari (feminine ta-fari).

Derivative verbs can be formed in two ways: either by adding the suffix -ta to the noun:

kunyata = to disgrace, to shame, from kunya = shame

or by combining a verb with a noun. The verb appearing most frequently in these combinations is yi = to do:

shawara = council - yi shawara = to consult

mamaki = surprise - yi mamaki = to be surprised.

Nouns may be combined with other verbs however:

sha wuya = to experience difficulties (sha = to drink, wuya = difficulty)

ji tsoro = to be afraid (ji = to feel, tsoro = fear), etc.

Reduplication and composition are also used in word formation in Hausa. Thus for example, the word launi = colour when reduplicated gives a new lexical item:

launi-launi = something variegated, many-coloured.

Composite words may consist of two nouns, or of verb plus noun:

jagaba = guide (formed from ja = to lead + gaba = front)

ubangida = owner, master, head of household (from uba = father + gida = house)

uwargida = mistress of household (from uwa = mother + gida = house)

ubandawaki = name of a post, position (from uba = father + dawaki = horses, pl. of doki).

Hausa also increases its vocabulary via extension of the meanings of existing words, thus:

inuwa = shadow has also come to mean 'protectorate'
reshe = twig, branch also means 'section or branch of a political party, trade union, etc.'

But the main source of lexical enrichment is borrowing from other languages - primarily from Arabic and English, though there are a few words borrowed from neighbouring Sudanese languages and from European languages other than English (see 45, 57, 61, 62).

Arabic provides most of the borrowings in Hausa. These have been taken partly from colloquial Arabic (Maghrebi) and partly from written Arabic, in which case the Hausa reflects more accurately the original Arabic spelling. Virtually all the vocabulary of trade and commerce is borrowed from Arabic:

attajiri = merchant (تَاجِرٌ)
dilali = middle-man, broker (دِلَّالٌ)
riba = profit, gain (رِبَاءٌ)

many abstract concepts:

adawa = enmity (عَدَاءٌ)
asiri = secret (سِرٌّ)
hankali = mind, reason (عَقْلٌ)

words connected with Moslem religion and ceremonial:

addini = religion (دِينٌ)
musulmi = Muslim (مُسْلِمٌ)
annabi = prophet (نَبِيٌّ)
addu'a = prayer (دُعَاءٌ)

many scientific terms:

nahawu = grammar (نَحْوٌ)
fi'ili = verb (فِعْلٌ)
hisabi = mathematics (حِسَابٌ) etc.

More recent borrowings from Arabic comprise political terminology:

mulki = government (مُلْكٌ)

wakili = deputy (وَكِيل)

siyasa = policy, politics (سِيَاسَة)

jam'iyya = political party (جَامِعَة)

Also from Arabic, Hausa has borrowed the numerals from twenty onwards. Some of these are formed with the help of the Arabic preposition gaira (غَيْر) = without; thus, twenty-nine is talatin gaira ɗaya - literally, 'thirty without one'. Instead of gaira, the Hausa word babu, with the same meaning, is also used.

The use of Arabic personal names among the Hausa dates from their conversion to Islam. Every Muslim Hausa has two names, a Hausa name and an Arabic one, this second name being used only on ceremonial occasions, and in religious ritual; in ordinary life, the Hausa names are used.

The Arabic names for the days of the week as used in Hausa are:

Lahadi	Sunday
Littinin	Monday
Talata	Tuesday
Laraba	Wednesday
Alhamis	Thursday
Jumma'a	Friday
Asabar	Saturday*

Recently, the flow of Arabic words into Hausa has greatly decreased, to be replaced as a source of new vocabulary by English, and English borrowings have penetrated all areas of Hausa public and everyday life.

The earliest and one of the biggest influxes of English words into Hausa comprises administrative terminology, nomenclature for official posts, documents, etc.

* Along with Asabar, Sati (< English 'Saturday') is also used.

gwamnati = government
firimiya = prime minister (< premier)
sakatare < secretary,
minista < minister
fasfo < passport
kofe < copy
rajista < register
ritaya < retire.

Hausa military terminology is also full of English borrowings:

soja < soldier
hafsa < officer
kanar < colonel
sintiri < sentry
bom < bomb
maci < march

The rate at which borrowings in the fields of technology, transport and engineering are increasing is particularly high:

inji < engine
gireda < grader
rediyo < radio
lantarki < electric
katafila < caterpillar = tractor
gareji < garage
taya < tire
sitiyari < steer
wili < wheel

Medicine and education are two more fields where the number of English borrowings is very high:

kolej < college
kos < course
lacca < lecture

laburare < library
sikolashif < scholarship
asibiti < hospital
nas < nurse
bandeji < bandage

Borrowings in the fields of finance and law:

balas < balance
inshuwara < insurer
lauya < lawyer
sama < summon

In politics:

miti < meeting
furofaganda < propaganda

In sport:

tim < team
kwaf < cup
gol < goal

Measures of length:

inci < inch
mil < mile
yadi < yard

In everyday life:

tebur < table
filo < pillow
kanti < canteen
lifi < leave
suwaita < sweater

The names of the months of the year are also borrowed from English:

Janairu	Yuli
Fabrairu	Agusta
Maris	Satumba
Afril	Oktoba
Mayu	Nuwamba
Yuni	Disamba

Chapter 3

Morphology

Hausa distinguishes the following autosemantic parts of speech: nouns, adjectives, numerals, pronouns, verbs and adverbs, and the following syntactic parts of speech: prepositions, conjunctions, particles and interjections.

The non-derived (primary) word in Hausa is not morphologically coded; that is, it cannot be identified by formal inspection as a noun, a verb or any other part of speech. To identify a word as one or another part of speech we have to consider its grammatical markers, if any, its function in the sentence and its combinatory relations with other words.

Within the framework of the sentence, words may appear either in their lexical form, or in linked form. In this latter case, the noun is modulated by the construct state markers - the suffixes -n (for masculine nouns) and -r (for feminine nouns):

littafin Audu = Audu's book (littafi, masc. gender, = book)

gonar uba = the father's field (gona, fem. gender, = field)

The construct state markers also have an independent (free) form: na (masc.) and ta (fem.):

ƙamus na Hausa = Hausa dictionary (ƙamus, masc. gender, = dictionary) rana ta biyu = the second day (rana, fem. gender, = day).*

In many respects, nouns and adjectives are close to each other: they share certain formative procedures (e.g. the mai- prefix), they both have the grammatical categories of gender and number, and have the same functions in a sentence. They differ, however, in the ways in which they can combine with other words. Thus, if the attributive in a sentence is an adjective, it can stand either before or after the word it qualifies. In the former case, the adjective takes the construct state marker:

babba = big; babban gida = big house

in the second case, the relation between qualifier and qualified is expressed by word-order alone:

mai-kyau = beautiful; gida mai-kyau = beautiful house.

If the attributive is a noun it can only stand after the word qualified which then receives the construct state marker:

gida = house; gidan uba = the father's house.

The numerals fulfil the same function in the sentence as other nouns. When a numeral is used as an attributive, however, it has to follow the word qualified, and, like an

* This marker is usually called the 'genitive copula'; see (244, pp. 47-57) for more detail. Because of the semantics of the word 'genitival', the term 'genitival link' (genitive copula) very often raises incorrect associations. Besides, 'genitivity' is only one of many meanings represented by this marker. I prefer to use the term *construct state marker* which is terminologically absolutely neutral as well as being highly informative: even in cases where one of the elements of the construction is not present, this marker shows that the represented element is not free, that is, it is constructionally bound.

adjective, in this position it does not take the construct state marker:

mace uku = three women.

Otherwise, however, numerals have much in common with nouns, although their function in the sentence is of course necessarily limited by their specific lexical meaning.

We shall now look at the various parts of speech and their grammatical properties.

THE NOUN

Hausa nouns are divided into two categories: primary nouns and deverbative nouns of action and state. This division is based on the fact that the two groups differ in their relationship to the conjugation system. Deverbative nouns are an indissoluble part of this system, while nouns belonging to the first group appear only sporadically in conjugated form as predicate. The deverbatives are treated in the chapter on the verb, as they are essential to an understanding of the conjugation system. Here it is enough to point out that deverbatives can fulfil all the functions of primary nouns in the sentence, as one might expect from their lexical content.

Nouns have the two grammatical categories of gender and number.

Hausa has two genders: masculine and feminine. Feminine nouns include

(1) most words ending in -a

fada = courtyard
rana = sun
wauta = stupidity

(2) all geographical terms (towns, countries, etc.)

(3) the names of the days of the week, irrespective of final

(4) the word mace = woman.

Masculine in gender are:

(1) almost all nouns not ending in -a

gado = inheritance

baki = mouth

ƙamus = dictionary

(2) some words ending in -a

ruwa = water

gida = house

kara = stem, stalk

wata = moon

guga = bucket, etc.

(3) nouns denoting male beings irrespective of final vowel:

uba = father

bawa = slave

lebura = worker

zakara = cock

likita = doctor, etc.

Some nouns vary in gender from one dialect to another: thus, iska = wind is feminine in the Kano dialect, and masculine in that of Sokoto. Some nouns denote beings of both sexes: thus,

kaka = grandfather/mother

agola = stepson/daughter.

There are two numbers in Hausa, singular and plural. The formation of the plural is an intricate and many-sided business; often a word has several plural forms which may be used indifferently or selectively:

shawara = council has plural forms shawarwari, shawarori, shawarce-shawarce

ƙasa = country has plural forms ƙasashe, ƙasaisai, ƙassai.

The most important ways of forming the plural are as follows:

(1) By suffix: the most frequently used suffixes being:

-a:

yaro = boy, pl. yara

haƙori = tooth, pl. haƙora

-ai:

dabino = date (fruit), pl. dabinai

balidi = backward pupil, pl. balidai

adudu = basket, pl. adudai

-aye:

kifi = fish, pl. kifaye

bebe = deaf-mute, pl. bebaye

-u:

basilla = big thorn, pl. basillu

dabara = plan, pl. dabaru

-una:

bante = loincloth, pl. bantuna

ɗaki = room, pl. ɗakuna

-wa:

annabi = prophet, pl. annabawa

-i:

hankaka = crow, pl. hankaki

barewa = antelope, pl. bareyi

-ki:

gona = field, pl. gonaki

(2) By reduplication, either total or partial, of the base; the ending may also be altered:

iri = sort, kind, pl. iri-iri

dambe = fight, pl. dambe-dambe

kitso = hairstyle, pl. kitsa-kitse

dangi = relative, pl. dange-dange

takarda = paper, pl. takardodi
ƙofa = door, pl. ƙofofi
tuta = banner, pl. tutoci
mota = car, pl. motoci
sha'ani = matter, affair, pl. sha'anunnuka
magana = word, pl. maganganu.

(3) By internal inflection; this - the so-called broken plural - is found in many languages belonging to the Semito-Hamitic family:

ƙirgi = skin, pl. ƙiraga
fuska = face, pl. fusaka
al'amari = matter, business, pl. al'amura

The broken plural may also be combined with reduplication:

ƙuduri = knot, pl. ƙudaddari

Formation of the broken plural may affect not only the vowels but also the consonants of the root:

ludayi = (name of a plant), pl. luwadu
sirdi = saddle, pl. siradda.

Suppletion also occurs:

wuri = cowrie shell, pl. kuɗi.

Occasionally, a second plural is formed from a plural, thus, doki = horse, broken pl. dawaki, from which another plural is formed by adding the suffix -ai: dawakai; similarly gona = field, pl. gonaki -- gonakai.

Some nouns have no plural forms. These are abstract nouns:

tsoro = fear
murna = joy
mugunta = evil
gaskiya = truth

names of various times of day and night:

maraice = evening
safe = morning

and the names of certain substances and objects:

alkama = wheat
ƙasa = earth
kura = dust
zuma = honey, etc.

Regular formation of the plural can be observed in the case of certain groups of nouns. Thus:

(1) nouns with the prefix mai- regularly change this to masu-:
mai-tafiya = traveller, pl. masu-tafiya

(2) nouns with the prefix ba- drop the prefix to form the plural and add the suffix -wa:
bahaushe = Hausa (person), pl. hausawa
bafade = courtier, pl. fadawa

(3) nouns with ɗan as a component change ɗan to 'yan in the plural:
ɗan kasuwa = merchant, trader, pl. 'yan kasuwa
ɗan iska = tramp, vagrant, pl. 'yan iska

(4) nouns with the ma- prefix and -i suffix denoting place of work or name of profession, change the suffix to -a:
maƙeri = smithy, pl. maƙera
marini = dyer, pl. marina
magini = builder, pl. magina

It is much more difficult to lay down rules for the formation of the plural of nouns morphologically less well defined than those collected under the above four headings. It can for example be said that concrete feminine nouns ending in the singular in -ya make their plural forms on the pattern of:

hanya = road, pl. hanyoyi
rijiya = well, pl. rijiyoyi

But akuya = goat, for example, a word belonging to this type, has, in addition to its 'regular' plural akuyoyi, a second plural form awakai, which is in fact more frequently used.

There are several more classes of nouns which form their plurals along certain regular patterns, but the rules governing these formations are a matter for specialised study rather than for a general description of the language such as the present work. (4, 30, 116) It remains to be added, however, that in the formation of the plural the tonal pattern of the base usually changes.

ADJECTIVAL NOMINALS

Hausa has both proper adjectival nominals - i.e. those which can only appear as attributes or as the predicate in a sentence - and mixed: i.e. those which can themselves be qualified, that is, substantivised.

Adjectival nominals proper include:

(1) Non-derivative adjectives, denoting

(a) colour:

fari = white
baƙi = black
ja = red
kore *and* algashi = green
shuɗi = blue
rawaya *and* yarani = yellow

(b) size:

babba = big
ƙarami *and* ƙankane = small
dogo = long
gajere = short

(c) certain qualities of an animate or inanimate object:

sabo = new

mugu = bad*

(2) adjectival nominals formed from abstract nouns of the type:
faɗi = breadth ← faffaɗa = broad
zaƙi = sweetness ← zazzaƙa = sweet
zafi = heat ← zazzafa = hot

The group of mixed adjectival nominals comprises:

(1) non-derivative nouns denoting qualities, characteristics, physical defects of human beings:
tsofo = old *and* old man
gurgu = lame *and* one who limps
Words in this group are often qualified rather than qualifiers.

(2) derivative nouns with the prefix mai-, formed from abstract nouns:
mai-kyau = beautiful
mai-ƙarfi = strong
These words may be qualified, but more frequently are themselves qualifiers or form the predicate.

Adjectival nominals are inflected for gender and number, though those with the mai- prefix have only one form for masculine and feminine:

mai-hankali = clever, masc. and fem.

the same goes for adjectival nominals ending in -a:

* Many non-derivative adjectivals could just as well be treated as substantives; for example, baƙi can mean not only 'black' but also 'blackness' and 'something black'; ƙarami means not only 'small' but also 'something small'. The nominals mentioned here however occur so very rarely in these meanings that we are quite justified in treating them as adjectives proper.

babba = big, masc. and fem.
ja = beautiful, masc. and fem.
faffaɗa = wide, broad, masc. and fem.

In all other cases, the feminine form of the adjectival nominal is formed from the masculine by means of the suffixes -a, -wa (-uwa), -ya (-iya):

baƙi = black, fem. baƙa
tsofo = old (masc.) - fem. tsofuwa
dogo = long (masc.) - fem. doguwa
shuɗi = blue (masc.) - fem. shuɗiya
gajere = short (masc.) - fem. gajeriya

Masculine and feminine adjectivals share a common plural form; those with the mai- prefix change this to masu- in the plural, but, in all other cases, formation of the plural form is characterised by the same wealth of patterns as we saw in the case of the nouns. Formation by addition of suffix alone is rare; as a rule, internal inflection is also present. The following are the main suffixes used in the formation of the plural forms of adjectival nominals (the examples illustrate the workings of internal inflection as well):

-u: gajeru (< gajere = short)
miyagu (< mugu = evil)
babbaƙu (< baƙi = black)

-aye: dogwaye (< dogo = long)
tsanwaye (< tsanwa = green)

-a: ƙanana (< ƙankane = small)
ƙarama (< ƙarami = small)
shuɗɗa (< shuɗi = blue)
kwarra (< kore = green)

-i: preceded by repetition of the consonant in the last syllable of the word:
sabbabi (< sabo = new)

rawayoyi (< rawaya = yellow)
shuɗoɗi (< shuɗi = blue)

The word babba = big has the suppletive plural manya.

Adjectival nominals agree in gender and number with the nouns they qualify. As an attribute, the adjectival usually precedes the word qualified, and, in this case, takes the construct state marker:

sababbin makarantu = new schools
ƙaramar gona = small field

Only in very few cases does the adjectival used attributively follow the word qualified.

As a predicate, the adjectival invariably follows the subject:

littafi sabone = the book is new
gida mai-kyaune = the house is handsome

Repetition of the adjectival suggests a weakening or incompletion of the quality denoted:

baƙi = black - baƙi-baƙi = blackish
sabo = new - sabo-sabo = almost new

THE NUMERALS

The Hausa numeral may be an attributive, in which case it follows the noun to which it refers. The noun is as a rule in the singular: thus, shekara bakwai = seven years where shekara = year is in the singular. The plural form may however also be occasionally used with an attributive numeral:

mutane biyu = two men

With the word guda = piece, item, the noun is also in the singular:

sule guda = one shilling

Guda may be placed between the noun and the attributive numeral:

doki guda biyar = five head of horses

In combinations formed by numeral plus personal pronoun, such as biyunku = two of you, ɗayamu = one of us, etc., the numerals biyu = two and ɗaya = one are substantivised and function as nouns.

Plural forms for the numerals exist, but these are scarcely ever used; in a few dialects the plural of goma = ten: gomiya, is used.

The numerals from one to ten are as follows:

ɗaya	1	shidda	6
biyu	2	bakwai	7
uku	3	takwas	8
huɗu	4	tara	9
biyar	5	goma	10

Beyond ten, the numerals are derived (derivative); from eleven to nineteen the connective particle sha is used:

goma sha ɗaya 11

goma sha biyu 12

goma sha uku 13 etc. up to nineteen

Here, the word goma is often left out: sha ɗaya, sha biyu, etc.

Although 18 and 19 can be made with the sha construction, it is more usual to express these two numerals in the negative form based on 20, thus:

ashirin babu biyu = 20 minus two

ashirin babu ɗaya = 20 minus one

and 28/29, 38/39, etc.

Compound numerals from twenty onwards are formed with the help of the conjunction da = and:

arba'in da biyar = 45

tamanin da shidda = 86

The names of the tens and the thousands are borrowed from Arabic:

arba'in = 40 (أَرْبَعُونَ)

saba'a = seven thousand (from Arabic سَبْع = seven)

Where all the components of a compound numeral are Arabic borrowings, the Arabic conjunction wa is used instead of the Hausa word da:

alif wa hamsaminya = a thousand and five hundred

Repetition of the numeral gives a distributive meaning:

ɗaya = 1, ɗaya-ɗaya = one by one

ashirin = 20, ashirin-ashirin = by twenties

THE PRONOUN

Hausa's kinship with the languages of the Semito-Hamitic family is most apparent in its pronominal system. In the singular, the Hausa personal pronouns have common Semitic markers: n for the 1st person, ka for the 2nd person masculine, ki for the 2nd person feminine. In the plural, the pronouns are formed with the help of the plural marker u, which is also shared with many Semito-Hamitic languages. Finally, in the 3rd person singular feminine, Hausa has the t marker which is common to many Chadic languages. Pronouns in Hausa have both gender - in the 2nd and 3rd person singular - and number. For ways of expressing gender in the possessive pronouns, see below.

Hausa is characterised by the presence of two series of dependent pronouns. Those of the first series are used in the conjugation of the verb and in the conjugation of the nominals; they will be considered in the section on the conjugation system.

The second series consists of the pronominal suffixes:

		Singular	Plural
1st person		-na	-mu
2nd person	masc.	-ka	-ku
	fem.	-ki	
3rd person	masc.	-sa	-su
	fem.	-ta	

These suffixes are used for various purposes. First of all, as the short forms of the possessive pronouns, they are joined to nominals bearing the construct state marker (n/r):

doki = horse - dokinka = your horse

allura = needle - allurarmu = our needle

an exception to this is provided by the 1st person singular where -na is added to masculine nouns (dokina = my horse) and -ta to feminine nouns (allurata = my needle), the consonant of the construct state marker being absent in both cases.

Secondly, combined with the masculine and feminine construct state markers, they provide the full form of the possessive pronouns; in the 1st person singular, the particle wa is used instead of the construct state marker:

		With masculine nouns	With feminine nouns
		Singular	
1st person		nawa	tawa
2nd person	masc.	naka	taka
	fem.	naki	taki
3rd person	masc.	nasa	tasa
	fem.	nata	tata

	With masculine nouns	With feminine nouns
	Plural	
1st person	namu	tamu
2nd person	naku	taku
3rd person	nasu	tasu

The first component of these pronouns indicates the gender of the thing possessed, while the second component specifies the number (in the case of 2nd and 3rd person singular, the gender as well) of the possessor:

doki naka = your (masc.) horse (masc.)

doki naki = your (fem.) horse (masc.)

allura taka = your (masc.) needle (fem.)

allura taki = your (fem.(needle (fem.)

The 1st person singular possessive pronouns nawa and tawa indicate the gender of the thing possessed only; the second component - wa - is neutral.

Thirdly, combined with the word kai = head, the pronominal suffixes produce word forms which function as reflexive pronouns. In all persons except the 1st person singular, kai takes on the construct state marker -n, whereby kai + -n > kan. In the 1st person singular kai takes the -na suffix without interposed marker:

		Singular	Plural
1st person		kaina	kanmu
2nd person	masc.	kanka	kanku
	fem.	kanki	
3rd person	masc.	kansa	kansu
	fem.	kanta	

This group of forms may have (a) reflexive sense proper:

ya ɓoyi kansa = he hid himself

kada ka zalunci kanka = don't ruin yourself

(b) oblique reflexive sense: to/for oneself:

ta sami littafin kanta = she got this book for herself

(c) improper reflexive sense, in which case the kai- compound may be preceded by the preposition da:

ni kaina *or* ni da kaina = I myself

Apart from the pronominal suffixes and the combinations in which they figure Hausa has the following pronominal series:

Independent personal pronouns

		Singular	Plural
1st person		ni	mu
2nd person	masc.	kai	ku
	fem.	ke	
3rd person	masc.	shi	su
	fem.	ita	

Pronouns in this series usually figure as the subject of a sentence:

ni ne = I am (it is I)

shi kuma ya yi jawabi = he also made a speech

Object personal pronouns

		Singular	Plural
1st person		ni	mu
2nd person	masc.	ka	ku
	fem.	ki	
3rd person	masc.	shi	su
	fem.	ta	

In combination with the so-called directional particle ma the object pronouns provide a third group of pronouns which may be called the directional or dative pronoun:

		Singular	Plural
1st person		mini	mana
2nd person	masc.	maka	muku
	fem.	miki	
3rd person	masc.	masa	musu
	fem.	mata	

Regressive assimilation appears in the 1st and 2nd person singular feminine forms, the vowel of the particle being affected by the vowel of the pronoun as follows:

ma + ni > mini, ma + ki > miki

in the 3rd person masculine singular, instead of mashi, masa is used (mashi is retained in the Sokoto dialect). In the 1st person plural, the pronoun itself is affected:

ma + mu > mana

(though again mamu is retained in the Sokoto dialect).

There are two kinds of demonstrative pronoun: the monosyllabic enclitics nan and can (= 'this' and 'that') follow the noun which takes the construct state marker

dokin nan = this horse

dokin can = that horse

while the demonstrative pronouns proper wannan = this (same form for both masculine and feminine, plural form waɗannan) and wancan = that (feminine form waccan, plural form waɗancan) precede the nouns to which they relate:

wannan doki = this horse

wancan doki = that horse

Like the demonstratives, the relative pronouns are formed in two ways:

(1) the pronoun da, which does not change for either gender or number, is placed immediately after the noun

to which it refers; the noun has the construct state marker:

labarin da na ji = the story which I heard

(2) da combines with the pronominal particle wa to form the relative pronoun wanda = who, which? (feminine wadda, plural waɗanda). It is placed after the noun to which it refers:

yaro wanda ya zo = the boy who came

The pronominal particle wa is involved in the formation of several other pronominal series and can also be used independently as an interrogative pronoun:

wa ka ke? = who are you?

Interrogative pronouns referring to an animate object are made by combining the particle wa with masculine and feminine connective forms (ne and ce), thus:

wane = fem. wace, pl. waɗanne = what?, what sort of?

Where reference is to an inanimate object, the particle me is used in combination with the same two connective forms:

mene *or* menene - fem. mece, mecece = what?

As a rule, all interrogative pronouns precede the word to which they refer:

menene ya faru? = What happened?

wace hanya ya tafi? = What way did he go?

Possessive interrogative pronouns follow the noun referred to, and are related to it by means of the construct state marker:

Dokin wanene ke nan? = Whose is this horse?

Gonar wa ta ke? = Whose field?

The particle wa is also used in the formation of the following pronouns:

wani = someone, anybody; fem. wata, pl. waɗansu

wane = such-and-such; fem. wance, pl. su wane

wani ... wani = one ... another: wani yaro ya fita, wani yaro ya zo = one boy went, another came

wani mutum: wani in combination with the word mutum = man means 'someone', ' a certain ...'; wani abu: in combination with abu = thing, wani means 'something'.

Finally, wa is used to make generalising pronouns:

kowa = every, each one, anyone (one form for both masc. and fem.)

These meanings are also expressed by the pronouns kowane: fem. kowace, pl. kowaɗane; kowanene: fem. kowacece, pl. kowaɗanene. These precede the noun to which they refer:

kowace mace = each woman

kowane lebura = each worker

They may be joined to the plural forms of the personal pronouns by means of the construct state marker:

kowanenmu = any (man) of us

kowacenmu = any (woman) of us

Other generalising pronouns are:

kome = all, whatever

and

duka = all

(these pronouns are not differentiated for gender or number).

The word duka can either precede or follow the word to which it is related. If it precedes, it takes the construct state marker and the word it refers to may be either singular or plural:

dukan gida = all the houses

mutane duka = all the people

dukansu = all of them.

Duka has a special intensive form:

dukka: dukkan ƙasashe = absolutely all countries

The word juna = each other is used in Hausa as a

reciprocal pronoun, which is used for all three persons without modification. The subject (agens) of a sentence containing this pronoun need not be animate; thus we have:

ƙetare da juna = to intersect (e.g. of roads) from ƙetare = to traverse

as well as

aminta da juna = to trust each other, from aminta = to entrust

raɗa da juna = to whisper to each other, from raɗa = to whisper

Juna is used both independently and in construct with the possessive pronoun in the person corresponding to the agens:

sun ga juna = sun ga junansu = they saw each other

Apart from its use as a reciprocal pronoun, juna also serves to indicate action in common, joint action:

zauna lafiya da juna = to live in peace together, from zauna lafiya = to live in peace

THE VERB

In their base form, most Hausa verbs end in -a:

ɗaura = to tie on to

kira = to call

Few verbs have a final vowel other than -a in the base form, e.g.:

ƙare = to finish

sani = to know

auku = happen, arise from

mutu = to die

so = to love

kai = to carry

hau = to rise

The final vowel of a base form is susceptible to change for

two reasons: in the formation of the derived verbal forms, and, secondly, in the expression of the relationships between the verb and the object of its action.

Hausa has the following derived forms of the verb: (1) causative; (2) intensive; (3) forms in -o; (4) forms in -e; (5) forms in -u.

(1) The causative is formed by adding the suffix -r/-ar to the verbal base (phonetic variants of this suffix are -s/-as and -d/-ad): the verb stands before the object and is accompanied by the preposition da:

fita = to go out - fitar (fitar da, fitad da) = to take out

sani = to know - sanar (sanar da, sanad da) = to inform, let know

Some monosyllabic verbs may dispense with the suffix -ar, and use the preposition da alone to express the causative:

ci = to eat - ci da = to feed

ji = to hear - ji da = to announce, cause to hear

As a rule, however, in the case of monosyllabic verbs and also in the case of the verbs tafi = to go and gaji = to be tired, the element -y- is interposed between the base and the causative suffix:

tafi > tafiyar = to lead

gaji > gajiyar = to weary (trans.)

ci > ciyar = to cause to eat, to feed

sha (to drink) > shayar = to give to drink

(2) The intensive form is made by reduplication. Here, either the first syllable of the root is repeated, e.g.:

danna = to squeeze - dandanna = to squeeze firmly

or the whole root, in which case consonantal clustering will produce either regressive assimilation:

buga = to beat - bugbuga > bubbuga = to beat mercilessly, to slaughter kama = to catch - kamkama > kakkama = to catch the lot

or dissimilation

kashe = to kill - kashkashe > karkashe = to slaughter (many people)

This form may also have iterative meaning:

aika = to send - a'aika = to send repeatedly

(3) The -o ending gives the following meanings to the verb: (a) action directed towards ... e.g.:

tafi = to go - tafo = to arrive

aika = to send - aiko = to send to someone

(b) performance of action on behalf of someone, e.g.:

saya = to buy - sayo = to buy for someone

nema = to look for - nemo = to search on behalf of someone

(4) With the -e final, the verb means (a) completion of action, action carried through to its limits or applied to the whole of the object:

ƙona = to burn - ƙone = to burn to the ground

duba = to look - dube = to inspect everything

If the verb is monosyllabic, the element -ny- is placed between the base and the ending:

ci = to eat - cinye = to eat everything up

sha = to drink - shanye = to drink everything up

(c) action directed from ...:

ɗauka = to take - ɗauke = to take and take away

ja = to drag = janye = to drag off

(5) The verbal form in -u has the following meanings:

(a) passive resultative:

dafa = to cook - dafu = to be cooked

(b) non-passive resultative:

karanta = to read - karantu = to be well-read

(c) potentiality of action; the potential forms in -u are usually used in negative constructions with a future tense form:

wannan littafin ba za su sayu ba = it is impossible to buy this book

(d) decausative:

canju = to change (from canja = to betray)

bazu = to spread, extend (intrans.) (from baza = to spread, tr.)

The way in which verbal action as related to an object is expressed depends on whether the verb is transitive or intransitive. In itself, this dichotomy depends first on the lexical meaning of a verb and secondly on its syntactic type - i.e. whether or not it can take an object.

As regards transitivity and intransitivity, Hausa verbs are divided into three groups. The first group comprises those verbs which are always transitive, irrespective of the presence or absence of an object:

ci = to eat

so = to love

ji = to hear

ɗauka = to take

further, verbs in causative form:

tsayad da = to place (from tsaya = to stand)

faɗad da = to drop (from faɗa = to fall)

sanad da = to inform (from sani = to know)

ji da = to announce (from ji = to hear)

The second group comprises verbs which are always intransitive:

tafi = to go

faɗa = to fall

zauna = to sit

bugu = to be beaten (from buga = to beat)

koyo = to learn (from koya = to teach)

The third group consists of verbs which can be either transitive or intransitive:

ɓoye = to hide (trans. and intrans.)

cika = to fill (trans.) and to be full (intrans.)

jira = to await someone/something (trans.) and to wait until a certain time (intrans.)

ƙare = to finish (trans. and intrans.)

Transitive verbs are divided into two groups - mutable and immutable. The former change their ending before an object, taking -i before a nominal and -e before a pronominal object:

ya ɗauka = he took (without specification of object)

ya ɗauke shi = he took him (object expressed by a pronoun)

ya ɗauki littafi = he took the book (object expressed by a nominal)

Immutable transitive verbs do not change their ending before an object:

ya kama = he caught (without object)

ya kama shi = he caught him

ya kama doki = he caught the horse

It must be made clear that in this context - positional inflection of verbal endings - we are speaking only of those inflectional changes that are reflected in the *written* language. Other changes take place in the Hausa verb, such as modification of tonal pattern and length of vowel. These phenomena affect all Hausa verbs in certain syntactic positions, not only those which are transitive and mutable.*

Verbal nouns (nouns of state or action) can be formed from

* See the division of Hausa verbs into 'grades' proposed by F. Parsons, a division based on the relationship between length of final vowel of a verb and its transitivity (179; see also 145, 191, etc.).

all Hausa verbs and from their derived forms. They are formed in several ways:

(1) by adding -wa to the verb:

gina = to build - ginawa

watse = to separate - watsewa

aiko = to send - aikowa

sayar = to sell - sayarwa

Two verbs form their verbal nouns by means of -ya:

tafi = to go - tafiya

gaji = to be tired - gajiya

(2) by conversion:

kama = to catch - kama

(3) by change of ending:

harba = to shoot - harbi

roƙa = to ask - roƙo

saya = to buy - saye

(4) by gradation of root vowel:

ɓoya = to hide oneself - ɓuya

ƙera = to forge - ƙira

(5) change of tonal pattern (in possible association with the previous two methods):

kira = to call

has high tone on the second syllable: the verbal noun kira has low tone here.

The verbal noun may be formed in two or three different ways from the same verb: thus, harba = to shoot has harbawa (with the -wa ending), harba (by conversion) and harbi (change of final). The choice of variant is conditioned by syntactic factors. (207)

In addition to verbal nouns, participles may also be formed from verbs. Participles from transitive verbs are active in meaning, and are formed by prefixing mai- to the verb (masu- in the plural):

na'urori masu saukake wahalan noma = machines alleviating difficulties in agriculture

From transitive verbs and from intransitive verbs with a reflexive meaning, passive participles are formed by repetition of the last syllable of the verb, with gemination of the consonant in this syllable and change of final vowel to -e:

kora = to drive away - korarre = exiled
rufa = to close, shut - rufaffe = closed
shuka = to sow - shukakke = sown
kunyata = to be ashamed - kunyatacce = ashamed
wanka = to wash oneself - wankakke = washed
kwanta = to lie down - kwantacce = laid down

From certain verbs, participles with an active meaning are formed in the same way:

fahimta = to understand - fahimtacce = understanding

If the base form of the verb ends in -e, this e is retained as final in the participle but the original -e of the verb is changed in what is now the penultimate syllable of the participle into -a-:

kare = to end - kararre = ended

From monosyllabic verbs, participles are formed as follows:

so = to love - soyayye = beloved
kai = to carry - kayayye = carried

All participles make their feminine and plural forms regularly, as follows: the feminine form has the suffix -iya, and the plural form has -u:

cikakke (masc.) = filled - fem. cikakkiya, pl. cikakku
dafaffe (masc.) = boiled, cooked - fem. dafaffiya, pl. dafaffu.

In addition to the simple (one-word) verbs, Hausa has compound verbs which are stable couplings of the verbs yi = to do and ji = to feel with various nouns:

yi hushi = to get angry (hushi = anger)

yi dariya = to laugh (dariya = laughter)

yi murna = to rejoice (murna = joy)

yi girma = to grow up (girma = growth)

yi waƙa = to sing (waka = song)

yi ƙoƙari = to try (ƙoƙari = effort)

ji tsoro = to fear (tsoro = fear)

ji tausayi = to grieve (tausayi = sorrow)

The verbal noun of such compound verbs is formed by giving the verbal component the construct state marker:

yi murna = to rejoice - yin murna

ji tsoro = to fear - jin tsoro

Hausa has eight aspectual-temporal forms, markers for which are provided by positional (adverbal) pronouns. In conjugation, it is only these markers which change - the verb itself remains unchanged. Eight groups of positional pronouns are used in the conjugation system: six for verbal conjugation and two for the nominal conjugation. Their form reflects on the one hand the character of the action (i.e. its relation to the moment of speaking: completion, non-completion, continuation) and on the other, the number and person of the agens. In addition, the 2nd and 3rd person singular forms reflect the gender of the agens:

ya ɗauka = he took (ya being the 3rd person masculine singular pronoun)

In verbal conjugation, the positional pronouns are associated with verbs; in the nominal conjugation they are associated with nominals. As a rule, it is verbal nouns that are conjugated (the second group of nominals) but sometimes non-deverbative nominals are also modulated by aspectual-temporal markers.

Pronouns of the 1st, 2nd and 3rd person, both singular and

plural, figure as components in each of the eight groups of positional pronouns (in the 2nd and 3rd person singular, gender is distinguished) and the indefinite-personal marker. It is customary to call the aspectual-temporal forms, as proposed by D.A. Ol'derogge, (164) after the 3rd person plural marker of each group:

su, sun, suka, za su, saa, su kan, suna, suka.

It is not possible to find a nomenclature that adequately reflects the grammatical significance of each aspectual-temporal form, mainly because here these grammatical meanings are expressed in non-partitioned form. A very tentative nomenclature, based on fundamental or, at least, frequency of usage, would be:

su = subjunctive mood*
sun = basic form of perfective aspect
suka = related form of perfective aspect
za su = future definite
saa = future conditional
su kan = habitual aspect
suna = basic form of durative aspect
suke = related form of durative aspect

The simplest is the su form, which involves no formants indicating duration or completion of action. The other seven forms all take various formants specifying state of action under these headings. The forms in each group are negated by means of specific negative particles.

Table 2 sets out these forms as represented in the conjugation of the verb gina = to build; the basic meaning of each aspectual-temporal form is appended:

* As John Lyons says: 'mood and tense may "intersect" in such a way that either one or the other label is equally appro priate' (J. Lyons, 'Introduction to Theoretical Linguistics', Cambridge University Press, 1968, p. 311).

Table 2

					Aspectual-Temporal Marker +
Number / Person / Gender	Name of Form	SU (Subjunctive Mood)	SUN (Perfective Aspect in Base Form)	SUKA (Perfective Aspect in Relative Form	ZA SU (Future Definite
Singular	1st p.	in gina	na gina	na gina	zan gina
		/so that/ I should build	I built	...[that] I built	I shall build
	2nd p. masc.	ka gina	ka gina	ka gina	za ka gina
	fem.	ki gina	kin gina	kika gina	za ki gina
	3rd p. masc.	ya gina	ya gina	ya gina	zai gina
	fem.	ta gina	ta gina	ta gina	za ta gina
Plural	1st p.	mu gina	mun gina	muka gina	za mu gina
	2nd p.	ku gina	kun gina	kuka gina	za ku gina
	3rd p.	su gina	sun gina	suka gina	za su gina
	Indefinite-Personal Marker	a gina	an gina	aka gina	za a gina
		/so that/ (they)* built	(they) built	/that which/ (they) built	(they) will build

* Here and in what follows, where the indefinite-personal form occurs, 'they' is bracketed, in order to distinguish this form from the *definite* 3rd person masc./pl.

Verb		Aspectual-Temporal Marker + Nominal	
SAA (Future Conditional)	SU KAN (Habitual Aspect)	SUNA (Durative Aspect in Base Form)	SUKE/SU KE (Durative Aspect in Relative Form)
naa gina	na kan gina	ina ginawa	ni ke ginawa
/if/ I build	I habitually build/built	I build	/that which/ I build
kaa gina	ka kan gina	kana ginawa	ka ke ginawa
kya gina	ki kan gina	kina ginawa	ki ke ginawa
yaa gina	ya kan gina	yana ginawa	ya ke ginawa
taa gina	ta kan gina	tana ginawa	ta ke ginawa
maa gina	mu kan gina	muna ginawa	mu ke ginawa
kwa gina	ku kan gina	kuna ginawa	ku ke ginawa
saa gina	su kan gina	suna ginawa	su ke ginawa
aa gina	a kan gina	ana ginawa	a ke ginawa
(they) will build /if.../	(they) habitually build/built	(they) build	/that which/ (they) build

The SU form indicates no more than performance of action. It is used to express:

(1) commands:

ka faɗa = speak, tell!

In this usage, the 2nd person pronoun, singular or plural, can be omitted. This is the normal way of forming the imperative in Hausa: the verb in its lexical form (base form) is used without adverbal pronoun but with a change of tone pattern (6, xi-xxvii);

(2) desirability that an action be performed:

kuna so ku gan ta = you want to see her (literally: you want that you saw her).

This is the basic application of the SU form, and it is this which by virtue of its optative nature, justifies our describing it as a mood. In sentences where it is preceded by the particle sai the SU form expresses the modal meaning of obligation:

suka ce sai su tafi gidansu = they said they had to go home

The SU form is negated by the particle kada:

kada ka nuna = don't show ...

The SUN form indicates:

(1) an action in general unrelated to the moment of speaking:

na sha taba = I smoke (general statement)

(2) an action which is already completed or which will necessarily be completed in the future:

Sun iso Nijeriya = they arrived in Nigeria (action completed in the past)

Saan nan ya ga, sun kusa dawowa daga wurin farauta, ya gudu = when he saw that they would soon return from the hunt, he ran away (where 'sun kusa dawowa' means, literally, 'they are approximating to returning', i.e. the action is bound to be completed);

(3) continuing action or state:
sun renaka = they hate you

Tense is determined by context: if the context is non-specific, the past tense is assumed.

The SUKA form is used:

(1) in relating something that is then in process of completion:
da muka gani ya shiga, muka tsaya wuri ɗaya = when we saw that he was coming in we were rooted to the spot
suka tafi, suka shiga daji = they set off and came into the forest

(2) in relative clauses after da = which:
mu raba kayanmu, da muka sata = we have to divide up the goods which we have stolen

As in the case of the SUN form, the tense is determined by context and is taken to be past tense in the absence of definite specification. SUN is used primarily in conditional clauses, SUKA in relative subordinate clauses.

In the singular, the formant -ka which appears in this form is retained only in the 2nd person feminine pronoun. In the Sokoto dialect, -nka appears instead of -ka: munka, sunka, etc.

The forms ZA SU and SAA both refer to future time. ZA SU consists of the verb za (which by itself means 'to go') and the short form of the pronoun. ZA SU can be called the form of definite future time:

daga nan za su wuce Bida = from here they will make for Bida

Apart from future time, ZA SU can also express the intention to perform some action or discharge an obligation:

za a yi cikakken binciken yadda haɗarin nan ya auku =
it is (will be) necessary to carry out a thorough investigation as to how this catastrophe came about

za ta dawo gida = she got ready to return home

zan faɗa maka, domin na yi abuta da kai =
I must tell you, why I am on friendly terms with you

The ZA SU form can also express potentiality, the possibility that such-and-such an action will be performed:

su kan nuna masa inda zai ajiye motarsa = as a rule they show him where he can park his car

In the 1st person singular, the form za ni > zan, and in the 3rd person singular masculine za ya > zai.

The conditional future form SAA is of rather rare occurrence in comparison with the other forms. Its main use is in subordinate conditional clauses or in principal clauses which have a conditional clause subordinate to them - i.e. in contexts where the action is in one way or another subject to conditions:

in Audu ya zo, kaa gan shi = if Audu comes, you will see him

in saa iya tafi yawo, na yi murna = if they can go for a walk, I shall be pleased

Supposition and conjecture provide another field in which the SAA form is used:

watakila kuma maa iya tafi yawo =
perhaps we too shall be able to go for a walk (here again certain conditions are presupposed under which it will be possible to go for a walk).

The pronouns in this conjugation are formed by the addition of the formant -a to the short form. The coalescence of this formant with the vowels of the pronoun has given rise to the forms with long vowels.

The SU KAN form is the so-called habitual form. It is made by combining the particle kan with the short form of the positional pronoun. The form indicates that performance of a certain action is usual or habitual:

su kan yi gaisuwa = they were in the habit of greeting each other

Only the context can fix tense here; as a rule, the context is one of either present or past time.

The SUN, SUKA, ZA SU, SAA, SU KAN forms are all negated by means of the negative particle ba, which is placed both before and after the verbal complex:

ba zan fadâ maka ba = I shan't tell you

In the 1st person singular and in the 3rd person singular masculine, the negative particle coalesces with the aspectual-temporal marker, i.e. ba + na > ban, ba + ya > bai:

ban yarda ba = I don't agree

bai zo ba = he didn't come

The nominal conjugational form SUNA expresses incompletion of action, continuation in a certain state, location in or at a certain place, etc. As a rule, this form refers to the present time, but it can also refer to an action or state in the past or future: the context will fix the tense to be used. The basic meaning is that of continuing action, of action in the process of performance.

The pronouns of the SUNA form are made by adding the formant -na to the short form of the pronoun. As a rule, it is verbal nouns that are conjugated according to the SUNA pattern, but examples can be found of first category nouns (i.e. not derived from verbs) being declined in this form:

Ana tsammani fasinjojin cikinsa sun dashi 700 =

I suppose there were about 700 passengers in it (the train)

29 suna asibitotin Ibadan = 29 people are in Ibadan hospital

wani mutum ya ji suna gardama = a man was listening to them quarrelling

Verbs consisting of verb plus noun can be used in the SUNA form:

wannan bak̃ar al'ada tana ba likitoci haushi =
this savage custom arouses the anger of the doctors
(ba haushi = arouse anger)

The pronouns in the SUNA form are often accompanied by nominals with prepositions (da = with, etc.):

ina da niyyar ... = I intend to ... (literally, 'I am with the intention')

yana cikin matsuwan rashin kud̃i = he found himself in straitened circumstances because of a lack of money

When the verbal noun in -wa is used in the SUNA form before a direct object, the -wa is dropped:

yana ginawa = he builds

but

yana gina gida = he builds a house

SUNA forms are negated by means of the negative particle ba; in the negative, the pronouns lose their -na formant, while na replaces ina in 1st person singular:

ba na ginawa = I do not build

ba ka ginawa = thou dost not build, etc.

In the SUNA paradigm, ba precedes the negated verbal complex only, that is, it is not recapitulated after it.

The SU KE nominal paradigm like the SUNA form indicates continuing action or state, but is employed mainly in relative constructions. The same nominal elements are used in the SU KE form as appear in the SUNA form. Examples:

abin da na ke son in yi magana = what I want to say ...
minene ya same ka, ka ke kuka = what has happened to you that you are weeping?
laifuffuka huɗu da a ke tuhumarsa = the four crimes of which he was suspected

The ke formant in this paradigm is often written separately from the pronoun in the short form, apparently because it has not yet lost its independent meaning as copula = to be, to be situated;* the SU KE form is not used in negative sentences. (4, p. 57)

To conclude our review of the Hausa verb system we must say something about the auxiliary verbs (89, 187) which 'to some extent help to make the system of "tenses" more flexible'. (207, p. 271) These auxiliaries supplement the meaning of the verb forming the predicate; at the same time, they retain the capability of being used independently in their own basic meanings. The predicate following such a verb is in the form of a verbal noun.

Thus, the juxtaposition of the verb taɓa = to touch indicates that the action has already taken place at some time or other:

ya taɓa yin kuka = he had already complained.

With a negative, this verb means 'never':

ban taɓa ganinsa ba = I have never seen him

The verbs riƙa and ɗinga = to hold, in juxtaposition with the predicate, indicate that an action already begun is continuing:

* In the SUNA and SU KE forms, C.H. Kraft writes both na and ke separately, treating them as specialised verbals. (109)

ya riƙa tafiya = he continued on (going)

the verb shiga = to enter has inchoative meaning:

suka shiga nema = they started carrying out searches

The fact that such-and-such an action has taken place before a certain moment is indicated by the verb riga/rigaya. In connection with this verb, the place of an object is taken by a subordinate cluase:

ya riga ya zo = he had already come (earlier)

THE ADVERB

Adverbs in Hausa are divided by meaning into several groups. Each group contains both primary and derivatory adverbs, the latter formed in various ways.

Most adverbs are formed by combining nominals and verbs with the particle da:

da gudu = running (from gudu = to run)

da sauri = quickly (from sauri = rapidity, speed)

da dare = by night (from dare = night)

da wuri = early (from wuri = early hour)

da yawa = many (from yawa = multitude)

The same particle also appears in the two adverbs:

bi da bi = continuously, uninterruptedly

nan da nan = at once

Adverbs of direction are made with the suffix -ci:

gabasci = to the east, eastwards (gabas = east)

yammaci = to the west (yamma = west)

arewaci = to the north (arewa = north)

kudanci = to the south (kudu = south)

Among the derivatory adverbs are those formed according to no definite pattern or model:

baki ɗaya = at the same time

babu shakka = without doubt, etc.

There is one group of words which can be used as adverbs of time and also as nominals:

gobe = tomorrow (adverb) and tomorrow (noun)
jiya = yesterday (adverb and noun)
bara = last year (adverb and noun)
bana = this year (adverb and noun)
kaka = dry season (adverb and noun)

Most of the non-derivative adverbs, that is the adverbs proper, are descriptive, specify the manner of action, or make appraisal of the action:

haka = in this way
kullum *and* koyaushe = constantly, always
tare = together
tilas = by force, forcibly
dole = necessarily
maza = quickly
banza = in vain
ainun = extraordinarily
lalle = it is necessary
labudda = doubtless, etc.

Another large group consists of adverbs of place:

nan = here
can = there
ciki = inside
waje = from the outside

of degree:

kadan = a little
ƙwarai = very

and of time:

yanzu = now
yau = today
da = formerly

We have done no more here than mention the basic and most frequently used adverbs. Attention should also be drawn to the group of intensifying adverbs, which are formally homogeneous, in that they are always disyllabic with the second syllable closed. They express positive or negative intensification of the action, the abruptness or the unexpected nature of the action, or other shades of meaning characteristic of the action:

ya tashi ƙazam = he got up suddenly
tsofo kutuf = a very old man
ya faɗi sharaf = he fell headlong
yana da zurfi zuɗum = it is very deep
sule yur zam ba ka = I'll give you shillings only (14)

THE PREPOSITION

Hausa has three types of preposition: simple, derivative and compound. The simple prepositions express motion towards something (ma, wa, ga, gare = into, to, towards), location (a = in, at), motion from (daga = from, out of), limitation (har = up to, as far as).

Derivative prepositions are, formally, nominals with the marker -n. They indicate the location of an object:

cikin = in (from ciki = stomach)
wurin = in (from wuri = place)
tsakanin = between (from tsakani = middle)
gaban = in front of (from gaba = breast)
bayan = behind (from baya = back)
kan = on (from kai = head)
bisan = on (from bisa = top)
karkashin = under (from karkashi = lower part)

Compound prepositions are formed from two simple prepositions: a kan *or* a bisan = on, a bayan = behind, etc. As a rule, they add nothing to the meaning of the simple prepositions forming them, and their instability makes them very liable to disintegration.

The compound preposition game da = about, concerning is stable.

THE CONJUNCTION

Conjunctions are mainly used as connecting links between the component parts of compound propositions, and will be treated in rather more detail when we come to analyse the structure of these propositions in Hausa.

As a connective between single words the conjunction da = and is used:

yana koyon karatu da rubutu = he is learning to read and write

In enumeration, this conjunction precedes each word:

yana da littafi da alkalami da takarda = he has a book, a pen and paper

Opposition or contrast is expressed by the conjunction ko = or:

kawo ma ni wani tukunya ko wani randa = bring me any sort of jug or pitcher

PARTICLES

The basic particles in Hausa are:

kuwa, kuma (or, ma) = indeed, as for, now ...:

Fillanin kuwa zarumawa ne = the Fulani, now - they are brave warriors

su kuma suna da yawa = well, there's a lot of them

su kuwa suka koma = they too came back

dai has very much the same meaning:

tun da farko dai mu biyar ne = to begin with, there were five of us

ko = even, whether:

wannan sheria ko ni ɗaya na isa = for this business even I by myself am enough

matsiyaci ba shi da komi, ko abinci = the poor man has nothing, not even food

a tanbayi matanshi, ko ta ga doki = let them ask his wife whether she saw a horse

INTERJECTIONS

Hausa has a large number of interjections. The commonest are:

to = there you are

to haka a ke = so there you are, that's how it was!

ashe = really, indeed

ashe wannan abin yabo ne = now really, this is worthy of praise!

kaito (or, kaico) alas!

akwai waɗansu wawayen mutane, kaito = there are, alas! stupid people

aha expresses satisfaction; oho suggests that the speaker does not wish to have anything to do with something or other.

Chapter 4

Syntax

Relations between the various components of a Hausa sentence are expressed by means of word order on the one hand and certain auxiliary words on the other. Of particular importance is the syntactic relation known as the construct state (*status constructus*). The morphological formation of the construct state was described above (p. 28); here we are concerned with its grammatical meaning.

It is customary to describe groups of words in Hausa linked by the construct state marker, as genitival constructions. But there is considerably more variety of relationship among the components of these constructions than is suggested by this name. The construct state marker may indicate possession:

gidan uba = father's house

a quality or property of an object:

babban gida = big house

cikakken bincike = thorough investigation

the purpose of an object:

alhawami na kamun wuta = tinder for getting fire

the relationship between the object specified in the conjugated form and the object of the action:

mutum yana kirawon yaro = the man calls the boy (literally, 'the man finds himself in the state of calling the boy')

the relationship between two parts of a composite predicate:

ta yi ƙoƙarin fita = she tried to go out

and there are a few other usages.*

If the construct state marker is attached to a word but is not marking a specific semantic connection between this word and other words in the sentence, the marker is acting as a definite article:

Audu ya ɗauki littafin = Audu took *this* book (already referred to)

Audu ya sa rigar = Audu put on *this* shirt (already referred to)

The construct state marker appears in various syntactic constructions in varying grammatical capacities. F. Parsons remarks that 'Hausa is above all a language of genitival constructions'. (178, p. 124)

THE SIMPLE SENTENCE

Simplifying the situation to some extent, we may say that in Hausa we find verbal sentences - that is to say, those sentences whose predicate is a combination of aspectual-temporal marker with a meaningful component - and non-verbal sentences - all other types.

The word order in a non-verbal sentence is: subject, the nominal part of the predicate, predicative particle (ne in the case of masculine nouns, ce in the case of feminine):

Audu malami ne = Audu is a teacher

* Y.K. Shcheglov distinguishes 16 different meanings of the genitive construction. (207, pp. 121-4)

Faɗimatu yarinya ce = Fatima is a girl

wannan gida ne = this is a house

wannan gida sabo ne = this house is new

yaro mai-hankali ne = the boy is intelligent

In verbal sentences, the normal word order is: subject, predicate, object:

mutane sun gina gida = the people built the house

The aspectual-temporal marker agrees in gender, person and number with the subject. If no subject is specified (e.g. if something already known is being referred to) agreement with the understood subject is still observed:

sun gina gida = they (the people) built the house

The minimal sentence is equivalent to its own predicate:

sun zo = they came

Where two objects are present in a sentence, they can be ordered in two ways:

(1) If the construction contains an indirect object denoting the recipient of the verbal action, this comes immediately after the predicate, followed by the direct object. The indirect object is introduced by the prepositions wa (before nominals) and ma (before pronominals):

uwa ta saƙa wa Audu suwaita = mother knitted Audu a sweater

uwa ta saƙa masa suwaita = mother knitted him a sweater

Verbs of giving take the indirect object without preposition:

Audu ya ba ni littafi = Audu gave me a book

(2) If the recipient of the action is not specified, the direct object is placed first followed by any other objective complement:

sun naɗa ka wakilinsu = they appointed you their representative

an rufe tukunya da murfi = (they) put the lid on the saucepan

A qualifier may either precede or follow the qualified:

ƙaramin yaro = little boy

wutsiyar doki = the horse's tail

Adverbial modifiers may be placed at the beginning or the end of the sentence:

kwana bakwai su kan yi irin wannan wasa =
they usually organise games like these in the course of seven days

aka sawo raguna guda uku, aka kawo da safe =
three sheep were bought and brought back in the morning

a kawo shi tilas = let him be brought by force

muka tafi tare da su = we set out together with them

This is the usual order of components in sentence. But Hausa is fond of inversion, and we shall now look at some of the more frequent examples of this. Inversion of the direct object means that it is transferred to a pre-predicate position:

wurin kwana zai nema = lodging for the night he must seek

When this happens, the normal position of the direct object may be occupied by an object pronoun agreeing with the direct object:

kayan aiki da tufafin duk za a ba da su kyauta ne =
tools and clothing, - all - will be given them - without charge (from an announcement in a newspaper)

When the dative (indirect) object is inverted the directional particle which introduces it remains in its normal place; that is, inversion affects the indirect object only:

shi a ke aza wa kaya = on it (i.e. on the camel) the things were loaded (169)

sarki ka ke faɗa wa wannan magana? = Is it to the King that you say such a thing? (207)

The sense part of the predicate - the component bearing the meaning - is also subject to inversion:

yana gida = he is at home

a gida ya ke = he is in the house (not elsewhere) (109)

Let us now look at different ways of expressing the various components of the sentence

The subject

The following parts of speech may act as subject:

(1) A noun:

iyayensa suka mutu = his parents died

(2) A personal independent pronoun: this happens in cases where it is felt necessary to stress, underline the subject, and the pronoun is then accompanied, as a rule, by an 'intensifying' or predicative particle:

shi kuma ya tafo nan = it was *he* who came here

ita ce ta buɗe taga = it was *she* who opened the window

The independent pronoun is not usually found as subject in sentences which do not have an emphasised pronominal component, as it is unmistakably recapitulated in the adverbal (positional) pronoun.

(3) A dependent pronoun where the identity of the agens is already known:

sun ga ƙananan yara = they saw the little boys

(4) Various other pronouns:

dukansu suka kewaye wurin nan = they all surrounded this place

waɗansu suka yi gudu = some fled

kowa ya san aikin tsabta a ƙasan nan ba ƙanƙanen aiki ba ne = everyone knows that the job of maintaining cleanliness in this region is no small task

(5) A numeral:

dayansu ya tafi = one of them set out

The predicate

In a non-verbal sentence, the predicate is a combination of a noun with the predicative particle (see above). There is however another type of non-verbal sentence - those formed with the help of the word akwai which is equivalent to English 'there is/are was/were':

akwai wani mutum a garin nan = there was/is a man in this town

akwai gida mai-kyau a kan titin = there is a beautiful house in this street

Akwai is not used with the aspectual-temporal markers, so the tense of a sentence containing it is non-specific. (34)

The sense of a verbal predicate may be expressed:

(1) by the simple verb:

ubana ya zauna nan = my father lived here

aiki ya kare = the work is finished

(2) by a compound verb:

yaro ya yi kuskure = the boy made a mistake

(3) by the noun of action, whether verbal

mutane suna jirammu = the people are awaiting us

or non-verbal

yana rangadi = he is travelling

(4) by a combination of auxiliary or modal verb/verbal noun with the base verb/verbal noun

ta yi ƙoƙarin fita = she tried to go out

yana son samu riba = he wants to get interest

mutane sun kasa shiryawa = the people could not agree

or with a non-deverbative nominal:

yaro ya kasa barci = the boy could not sleep

(5) where there is an aspectual-temporal marker in the SUNA form, by a combination of the preposition da with a nominal denoting (a) a quality or property:

yana da kyau = he is handsome

yana da nauyi = he is heavy

and (b) ownership of something:

yana da gida = he has a house

The object

The object can be a noun or pronoun:

ya ɗauki littafi = he took the book

mutum ya buge shi = the man hit him

The verb may have two objects:

suna so a maida shi sule guda = they want to return a shilling to him

suka cika jaka da ciyawa = they filled the bag with grass

In the latter example, the second object is connected to the verb by means of a preposition. Prepositions are also used to express direction of action towards an object:

muna roƙon a gina mana makaranta = we ask that a school should be built for us

ya gaya wa kotu yadda aka yi sacin = he told the court how this theft was carried out

The attribute

Any noun or pronoun can be an attributive in Hausa, and when so used, the noun or pronoun is, as a rule, in the construct state with the noun qualified:

suka samo fatar buhu guda biyu = they found two leather bags mutanen ƙasar nan suka gama kan su = the inhabitants of this region have united

su yi laifin satar magani a asibiti =
they stole medicine from the hospital (literally, they committed the crime of theft of medicine from the hospital).

If the qualifier is a pronoun preceding the noun qualified, the connection is expressed by word order only:

aka buɗe wannan asibiti nasu = this hospital was opened

sun fara nuna waɗannan kayayyaki nasu = they began to show their belongings

Pronominal and adjectival modifiers agree with the word they qualify in gender and number

The adverbial modifier

An adverbial modifier (whether a single word (usually an adverb) or a group of words) can stand at either the beginning or the end of the sentence, irrespective of the nature of the actual parts of speech involved. Examples of adverbial modifiers:

ya bada ƙanena can = he sent my younger brother there

muka tafi da safe = we set out in the morning

Examples of composite modifiers (noun + preposition or noun + adverb):

har yanzu dai 'Watan Russia' yana ta kewaya duniya =
since then, the 'Russian Moon' has been circling the earth

A wannan Gaskiya kun karanta labari = in this 'Gaskiya' you have read the announcement ...

ba ya gajiya har abada = he never gets tired

ina yin kuka saboda gajiya = I wept for tiredness

sau da yawa mai duban hanya ya kan wuce ta = many times the track-man has made the rounds of it (the railway)

THE COMPOSITE SENTENCE

The complex sentence

In Hausa there are two types of complex sentence:

(a) without a conjunction:
ta tamlayeni labari duka, na faɗa mata waɗansu = she asked me about everything, I told her something or other

(b) with the adversative conjunction amma = but:
ana iya tura doki zuwa rafi, amma ba za ka iya tilasta shi ya sha ruwa ba = you can take a horse to the river but you can't make it drink water
en'e na iya ce masa ya yi ritaya, amma sai am ba shi sanarwa ta wata shida = the local administration can tell him he should retire, but (they) have to give him six months' notice.

The compound sentence

All the components of a compound sentence, whether principal clause or subordinate clauses, retain the same word order as is normal for simple sentences. The only differences in structure are that, as a rule, subordinate clauses have words which link these clauses to the principal clause. Sometimes the principal clause itself contains one or more particles indicating that a subordinate clause is to be introduced. One principal clause is often accompanied by several subordinate clauses which are interconnected either by coordination or by ordered sequence.

The main types of subordinate sentence

Subordinate relative clauses are connected to the principal clause by the relative pronouns da and wanda = who, which, that. Relative clauses may follow the principal clause or be inserted in it after the word to which they refer. In the following examples, the subordinate relative clause follows the principal clause:

ya kira wota na baiwansa, da ta ke yin maganan Hausa =
he summoned his bondwoman who knew the Hausa language

ya gaya mana wuraren da za mu ziyarta = he told me about places which we ought to visit

In the next examples the relative clause is inserted in the framework of the principal clause:

muna roƙon dokar ta bayyana duk mutumin da ke da kare ya ɗaure abinsa a gida = we ask that a decree should bind every man who owns a dog to tie it up at home (i.e. that every man should be obliged by law to ...)

bakin titi da ta bi yana cike da mutane =
the pavement of the street along which she was walking was crowded with people

Subordinate complementary clauses always follow the principal clause. As a rule no conjunction is used with these:

mutane suka gan, barewa ta faɗi = the people saw that the antelope fell

yana tsoro kada a sace su ne = he was afraid lest (they) be stolen

However, the conjunction cewa = that may also be used:

an kuma ba da labari, cewa ruwa ya wanke waɗansu kadarki =
it is also reported that the water has swept away several bridges

kowa ya sani cewa duk duniyan nan babu sana'ar da ta fi noma wuya = everyone knows that there is no heavier work on earth than agriculture

An interrogative shade of meaning is given to the complementary clause by particle ko = whether

suka tafi domin su gani ko ya ƙuna ne = they went to see whether he had not been burnt (scorched)

kafin ya yanke wannan hukunci sai da ya tambayi M. Muhammadu ko yana da wata magana = before passing sentence, he asked M. Muhammad whether he had anything to say

Subordinate clauses of time, introduced by the conjunctions da, idan, lokacin = when ..., tun da = since, bayan = after, usually precede the principal clause. Where a subordinate temporal clause is present, the principal clause often contains the particle sai which is here not translated and serves merely to mark the transition from one action to another:

da suka tafi ɗakin sai suka tarar uwarsa ba ta nan a ɗakin = when they came into the room they discovered that their mother was not there (in that room)

bayan an yanke hukunci sai aka ɗauke shi cikin mota = after sentence had been passed, he (the prisoner) was put in the car

if, however, the predicate of the subordinate clause beginning with sai is in the subjunctive, then sai indicates obligation:

idan yaran suka shekara bakwai sai a sa su a makaranta = when boys have completed their seventh year, they are sent to school

Subordinate temporal clauses beginning with the conjunction har = till, until, as long as, are placed after the principal clause:

mutanensa suna binsa, har ya iso kusa da sarki =
his people followed him, as long as he had not approached
the emperor (until he approached the emperor)

su ke ciyar da shi su ke shayar da shi har sai yaro ya zama
mutum sosai = they give him food and drink until the boy is
a grown man

Subordinate conditional clauses are connected to the principal clause which they normally precede by means of the conjunctions in, kadan = if:

kadan ka samesa ka tafi garinka da shi = if you find him,
go to your town
together with him

Subordinate causal clauses and subordinate clauses of purpose normally follow the principal clause and are connected to it by the conjunctions don, domin = so that, in order that, as:

aka yi murna da ganinsu, don da ana tsammanin an kashe su =
(they) rejoiced at the sight of them as (they) had reckoned
that (they) had killed them

mutane da yawan gaske suka taru a kotu don su ji hukuncin
da za a yanke = in fact, many people had assembled in the
court to hear the sentence which (they)
were bound to pronounce

sun kafa jam'iyarsu ne, domin su yaƙo wa kansu kyawawan
ƙa'idodin aiki da albashi mai maiƙo =
they set up their trade union so as to fight for an
improvement in conditions of work and an increase in wages

In subordinate clauses of purpose or intention which are not introduced by a conjunction, the predicate is in the subjunctive mood:

mun zo mu faɗa maka wannan = we have come (in order) to
tell you (of) this

Subordinate clauses of cause introduced by the conjunction sabo da = because of this, may precede the principal clause:

sabo da ambaliyan ruwa ma an rufe tashar motar Sakkwato = because of the floods the car-park in Sokoto has been closed

Subordinate clauses of manner are also met with but rather less frequently than those we have considered above. As a rule, such clauses are connected to the principal clause by the conjunction yadda = how, in what way:

ya gaya wa kotu yadda aka yi sacin = he told the court how the theft had been carried out

Within the limits of this study it has been possible to give no more than the barest outline of Hausa syntax. For those readers who wish a more detailed account of the subject we recommend the following works which offer a thorough treatment of Hausa syntax from various theoretical standpoints: 35, 36, 53, 80, 102, 180, 207, 243. Other works mentioned in the Bibliography should also be consulted.

Texts

TEXT I

Asalin hausawa an ce, waɗansu mutane ne, wa da kane, su ka zo daga kasal larabawa da matan su biu. Su ka zamna wani jeji kusa da kasal barno, sunansa gabi, su ka yi bukoki, su ka yi shimge, su na halbin namun jeji, don su ma-halba ne. Yau, mutane kuwa su na zua daga barno, su na sayasayar nama, kuma su na zua daga wasu gurare, su na sayasaya, har gun nan ya zama gari-gari. Su na nan, har matar kanen nan ta haifi ya, su ka sa ma ta suna fatsima, amma su na yi ma ta lakabi dauratu da larabci, shi ne kewaya, kaman sun ce, su na yin kewayal duniya, har su ka zo gabi su ka haife ta.

Text taken from:
A. Mischlich: Über Sitten und Gebräuche in Hausa.
I. Asalin Hausawa ('MSOS', X, III Abt., 1907, p. 155)

Translation

It is said that the origin of the Hausa was thus. Some people, an elder brother and a younger brother, came from Arab countries with their wives. They settled in a wild place not far from the country of Bornu. This place was called Gabi. Here they built huts and put up a fence. They hunted wild animals, because they were hunters. People came from Bornu and from other places and bought meat from them. In the end, the place was turned into a town. They lived there until the wife of the younger brother bore a girl. To this girl they gave the name Fatsima and as well as this, the nickname Daurata which means 'circle' in Arabic. They said that they had wandered about in the world until they came to Gabi and this girl was born.

TEXT II

Dubban mutane suka haɗu a Kwali ta ƙasar Abuja domin shagalin nuna amfanin gona wanda En'e ta Abuja ta shirya....

Sarkin Abuja da sauran sarakuna, su ne suka fara kewaya dukan kayayyakin da aka tara don nunawa. Am fara nuna amfanin gona da sauran sana'o'i tun daga ƙarfe sha ɗaya da rabi na rana ne. To, daga nan kuma sai alƙalan wannan wasa suka dudduba abubuwan da aka tattara don su ga waɗanda suka cancanta su sami kyauta. Bayan da alƙalai suka ƙare dubawa, sai kuma aka shiga rarraba kyauta ga waɗanda suka ci. A nan ne sarkin Abuja ya roƙi sarkin Kafi don ya rarraba kyauta ga mutanen da suka ci nasara.

Taken from the newspaper 'Gaskiya ta fi kwabo'
892, 20/III-59, Sh.3.

Translation

Thousands of people gathered together in Kwali (Abuju region) at an exhibition of agricultural production, which was prepared by the local administration of Abuju....

The chief* of Abuju and other leaders began to inspect

* sarki = (1) leader, emperor; (2) any chief, manager, government representative.

everything that was collected for demonstration. At half past eleven a.m. (they) began to exhibit agricultural production and the production of several crafts. The members of the jury at once inspected the objects which were collected together here, in order to decide what was deserving of a prize. After they had finished (they) began to distribute prizes among those who had won. The chief of Abuju turned to the chief of Kafi with a request that he should hand out the prizes to those people who gained victory.

Annotated glossary of words occurring in the texts

The glossary, which is in alphabetical order, contains all the words which appear in the two sample texts. Words are given in both their basic form and the form in which they appear in the text.

ABBREVIATIONS

sing.	= singular
pl.	= plural
fem.	= feminine gender
masc.	= masculine gender
pers.	= person
intens.	= intensifying form
pron.	= pronoun
con. st. m.	= construct state marker
sh.	= shortened form
suff.	= suffix

a	at, in (prep.)
abu	thing, object
	abubuwa-n: abubuwa pl. of abu; -n con. st. m.
aka	indefinite personal pron. in SUKA form
	(aka tara = (they) collected)

alƙalai — see alƙali

alƙali — judge
alƙala-n: alƙalai pl. of alƙali; -n con. st. m.; before -n the suff. -ai loses its second component -i

am — see an

amfani — profit, gain
amfani-n: -n con. st. m.
amfanin gona agricultural production

amma — but (conjunction)

an — indefinite personal pron. in SUN form
am: an > am before f (am fara - (they) began)

asali — origin
asali-n: -n con. st. m.

Balarabe — Arab
Larabawa pl. of Balarabe

Bahaushe — Hausa person
Hausawa pl. of Bahaushe

bayan — after
bayan da after

biu — two

buka — hut
bukoki pl. of buka

bukoki — see buka

cancanta — to deserve

ce — to speak

ci — to win

da — (1) who, which; (2) and (conjunction); (3) with (prep.); (4) kusa da - not far from; (5) bayan da - after; (6) da larabci - in Arabic

daga — (1) from, out of (preposition); (2) tun daga - with (preposition); (3) daga nan - at once

dauratu — proper name

ɗaya — one

sha ɗaya sh. form of goma sha ɗaya - eleven

domin — because of (preposition)

don — (1) for, in order that; (2) because

duba — to look at

dubawa - inspection; -wa - deverbative noun suffix; dudduba intens. form of duba

dubban — see dubi

dubi — thousand

dubban: dubbai pl. of dubi; -n con. st. m.

dudduba — see duba

duka — all

duka-n: -n con. st. m.

duniya — world

En'e — local administration (Engl. Native Administration)

fara — to begin

ga — (1) to see; (2) directional particle (ga mutane - to people)

gari — town

gona — field; amfanin gona - agricultural production

gu	place
	gu-n: -n con. st. m. gurare pl. of gu
gurare	see gu
haɗu	to assemble (intrans.)
haifa	to give birth to
	haife: haifa > haife before pronominal object
	haifi: haifa > haifi before nominal object
haife	see haifa
haifi	see haifa
halbin	halbi - verbal noun of halba = to shoot; -n con. st. m.
har	as long as, until
Hausawa	see Bahaushe
jeji	desert place, wilderness
ka	see suka
kaman	like, in the same way as
kane	younger brother
ƙare	to finish
ƙarfe	hour, time
kasa	see ƙasa
kasal	see kasa
	kasa-l: -l con. st. m.
ƙasa	country, region
	ƙasa-r: -r con. st. m.
kaya	burden, weight
	kayayyaki-n: kayayyaki pl. of kaya; -n con. st. m.
kayayyaki	see kaya
kewaya	circle
	kewayal: -l con. st. m.

	yi kewaya (1) to circle, turn round; (2) to go round
kuma	(1) emphatic particle; (2) and (conjunction)
kusa	not far
kuwa	emphatic particle
kyauta	prize
lakabi	nickname
Larabawa	see Balarabe
ma	directional particle (ma ta - to her)
mace	woman
	mata-n: mata pl. of mace; -n con. st. m.
na-halba	see ma-halbi
ma-halbi	hunter
	ma-halba pl. of ma-halbi
mata	(1) wife; (2) see mace
mutane	see mutum
mutum	man
	mutane-n: mutane pl. of mutum; -n con. st. m.
na	full form of con. st. m. for masculine nouns
nama	meat
	namu-n; namu pl. of nama; -n con. st. m.
	namun jeji - wild beasts
nan	(1) this; (2) there; (3) a nan, daga nan - right there, straight off
nasara	victory
	ci nasara - gain the victory
ne	predicative particle

nuna	to show, exhibit
	nuna-wa - showing, demonstration: -wa suff. deverbative noun; shagalin nuna - exhibition
raba	to divide
	rarraba - to distribute (intens. of raba)
rabi	half
rana	day
rarraba	see raba
roƙa	to ask
	roki: roƙa > roƙi before a nominal object
roƙi	see roƙa
sa	to put
	sa nuna - to give a name
sai	particle denoting sequence (transition from one state or action to another)
sami	to receive
sana'a	craft
	sana'o'i pl. of sana'a
sana'o'i	see sana'a
sarakuna	see sarki
sarki	leader, chief; 'sarki'
	sarki-n: -n con. st. m.
	sarakuna pl. of sarki
saura	others, the rest
	saura-n: -n con. st. m.
sayasaya	intens. of saya = to buy; sayasayar: -n con. st. m.
sha	connective particle in formation of composite numbers: goma sha ɗaya or sha ɗaya - eleven

shagali — matter, business, affair
  shagalin nuna - exhibition

shi — pron. 3rd pers. masc. sing.
  shi ne - this is (see ne)

shiga — to begin, to set about doing something

shimge — fence

shirya — to prepare, make ready

su — (1) pron. 3rd pers. pl.; (2) pronominal suff. denoting possession

suka, su ka — pron. 3rd pers. pl.

sun — pron. 3rd pers. pl.

su na — pron. 3rd pers. pl.

suna — name; suna-n-sa - his name: -n con. st. m. -sa pronominal suff. denoting possession

ta — (1) pron. 3rd pers. fem. sing.; (2) full form of con. st. m. with fem. nouns

tara — to gather
  tattara - to gather together (intens. of tara)

tattara — see tara

to — so, well, OK (exclamation)

tun — tun daga - with (preposition)

wa — elder brother

waɗansu — see wani

waɗanda — see wanɗa

wanɗa — who, which, that; waɗanda pl. of wanɗa

wani — a certain, another
  waɗansu, wasu pl. of wani

wannan — this

wasa — competition

wasu — see wani

ya	(1) pron. 3rd pers. masc. sing.;
	(2) daughter
yau	emphatic particle: 'you see ...'
yi	to do
	yin: -n con. st. m.
zamna	to settle in
za	to go
zo	to come
zua	arrival

Bibliography

ABBREVIATIONS

'ACAfrL'	'Third Annual Conference on African Linguistics'. (Indian Univ.), 7-8 April 1972. Indiana University Publications, Africa Series 7. Bloomington, 1974.
'AES'	'Afrikanskii etnograficheskii sbornik'. Trudy Instituta etnografii AN SSR, Novaya seriya. Moscow - Leningrad.
AF	Afrikanskaya Filologiya. Moscow, 1965.
'Africa'	'Africa'. Journal of the International African Institute. London.
'AIS'	'African Language Studies'. London.
'AnL'	'Anthropological Linguistics'. Bloomington. Indiana.
'AO'	'Archiv Orientalni'. Prague.
'AS'	'Afrikanistische Studien', hrsg. von J. Lukas. Berlin, 1955.
'ASK'	'Afrikanische Sprachen und Kulturen'. - Ein Querschnitt (Festschrift Johannes Lukas). Hamburg, 1971.

'AÜ'	'Afrika und Übersee'. Berlin.
'FO'	'Folia Orientalia'. Krakow
GLECS	Comptes Rendus du Groupe Linguistique d'Études Chamito-Sémitiques. Paris.
'HN'	'Harsunan Nijeriya'. Centre for the Study of Nigerian Languages. Bayero University College. Kano
'HS'	'Hamito-Semitica'. The Hague - Paris, 1975.
'JAL'	'Journal of African Languages'. Hertford.
'JWAL'	'Journal of West African Languages'. London.
'Lang.'	'Language'. Journal of the Linguistic Society of America. Baltimore.
'Linguistische Studien'	'Linguistische Studien', Reihe A. Arbeitsberichte 64. Sozialer Wandel in Afrika und die Entwicklung von Formen und Funktionen afrikanischer Sprachen. Berlin, 1980.
'LProbl.'	'Language Problems of Developing Nations'. New York, 1968.
'PChL'	'Papers in Chadic Linguistics'. Papers from the Leiden Colloquium of the Chadic Language Family. Leiden, 1977.
'PF'	'Problemy filologii'. Uchenye zapiski. Izd. 'Mezhdunarodnye otnosheniya'. Moscow, 1967.
'RO'	'Rocznik Orientalistyczny'. Warsaw.
'SAfrL'	'Studies in African Linguistics'. Los Angeles.

'SE'	'Sovetskaya Etnografiya'. Moscow.
'SKM'	'Statistiko-kombinatornoe modelirovanie yazykov'. Moscow - Leningrad, 1965.
'VAF'	'Voprosy afrikanskoi filologii'. Moscow, 1974.
'Word'	'Word'. Journal of the International Linguistic Association. New York.
'WPPh'	'Working Papers in Phonetics'. Phonetic Laboratory, University of California. Los Angeles.
'ZES'	'Zeitschrift für eingeborenen Sprachen'. Berlin.
'ZPhon'	'Zeitschrift für Phonetik, Sprachwissenschaft und Kommunikationsforschung'. Berlin.

1 Abraham, R.C. 'A Modern Grammar of Spoken Hausa'. London, 1941.

2 Abraham, R.C. 'An Introduction to Spoken Hausa'. London, 1940.

3 Abraham, R.C. 'Hausa Literature and the Hausa Sound System'. London, 1959.

4 Abraham, R.C. 'The Language of the Hausa People'. London, 1959.

5 Abraham, R.C. 'The Principles of Hausa'. Kaduna, 1934.

6 Abraham, R.C., and Malam Mai Kano. 'Dictionary of the Hausa Language'. London, 1949 (2nd edn, London, 1962).

7 Bagari, D.M. A note on the base form of the Hausa verb. 'SAfrL', 1975, 6 (3), 239-48.

8 Bagari, D.M. Dangantakar Hausa de Harsunan Afrika. (The relationship of Hausa with the tongues of Africa). 'HN', 1972, 2, 42-5.

9 Bagari, D.M. Lexicalist hypothesis and Hausa. 'SAfrL', 1971, 2, 197-216.

10 Bagari, D.M. NP complementation in Hausa. 'ALS', 1972, 13, 32-51.

11 Bagari, D.M. Reanalysing the Hausa causative Morpheme. 'PChL', 1-10.

12 Baikie, W.B. 'Observations on the Hausa and Fulfulde Languages'. London, 1861.

13 Baldi, S. 'Systematic Hausa Bibliography'. Rome, 1977.

14 Bargery, G.P. 'A Hausa-English Dictionary and English-Hausa Vocabulary'. (With some notes on the Hausa people and their language, by D. Westermann.) London, 1934.

15 Bargery, G.P., and Lloyd, J. A note on pronunciation of Hausa. 'Bulletin of the School of Oriental and African Studies'. London, 1926, 3 (4), 721-8.

16 Barth, H. 'Sammlung und Bearbeitung Zentral-Afrikanischer Vokabularien'. Vols I-III. Gotha, 1862-6.

17 Brauner, S. Bemerkungen zum entlehnten Wortschatz des Hausa (Yorubalehnwörter im Hausa). Mitteilungen des Instituts für Orientforschung. Berlin, 1964, 10 (1), 103-7.

18 Brauner, S. and Ashiwaju, M. 'Lehrbuch der Hausa-Sprache'. Leipzig, 1965.

19 Carnochan, J. A Study of Quantity in Hausa. 'Prosodic Analysis'. London, 1970, 91-103.

20 Carnochan, J. 'Gemination in Hausa. Studies in Linguistic Analysis' (Special Volume of the Philological Society). Oxford, 1957, 149-81.

21 Carnochan, J. Glottalization in Hausa. 'Transactions of the Philological Society'. Oxford, 1952, 78-109.

22 Churma, D.G. Is Hausa a Suprasegmental Language? 'Ohio State University Working Papers in Linguistics'. Columbus, 1975, 20, 106-15.

23 Cohen, M. La question de la parente du Haoussa (Soudan Français). 'GLECS', 1934, 2, 1-3.

24 Cowan, J.R. and Schuh, R.G. 'Spoken Hausa'. Ithaca, New York, 1976.

25 Dalby, D. The noun GARII in Hausa: a semantic study. 'JAL', 1964, 3 (3), 273-305.

26 Delafosse, M. 'Manuel de la langue Haoussa'. Paris, 1901.

27 Dirr, A. 'Manuel pratique de la langue haoussa'. Paris, 1895.

28 Dresel, L. Some phonological aspects of the acquisition of Hausa. 'SAfrL', 1977, 8, Suppl. 7, 23-31.

29 Dressler, W. 'Studien zur verbalen Pluralität' (Hausa - SS. 95-101). Vienna, 1968.

30 Dunn, E.F. Hausa plurals: a stratificational restatement. 'ACAfrL', 171-95.

31 D'yakonov, I.M. 'Semito-khamitskie yazyki. Opyt klassifikatsii'. Moscow, 1965.

32 East, R.M. 'Hausa spelling'. Zaria, 1953.

33 Essen, O., von. Implosive Verschlusslaute im Hausa. 'AU', 1962, 45 (4), 285-91.

34 Eulenberg, J.B. A new look at the predication particles in Hausa. 'SAfrL', 1971, 2 (2), 105-15.

35 Eulenberg, J.M. Complementation phenomena in Hausa. PhD diss., University of California, San Diego, 1972.

36 Eulenberg, J.B. and Ritter, J.T. 'A Generative Characterisation of the Subjunctive in Hausa'. Center for Applied Linguistics, Washington, DC.

37 Feyer, U. Haussa als Verkehrssprache. 'ZPhon', 1947, 1 (3), 108-29.

38 Fikhman, B.S. Materialy k izucheniyu glagola v yazyke Hausa. 'AES', 1963, 5, 222-58.

39 Fikhman, B.S. Vydelenie pervogo morfologicheskogo tipa v

yazyke Hausa po algoritmu statistiko-kombinatornogo modelirovaniya. 'SKM', 189-95.

40 Fikhman, B.S. Vydelenie vtorogo morfologicheskogo tipa v yazyke Hausa po algoritmu statistiko-kombinatornogo modeliroveniya. 'SKM', 275-85.

41 Frajzyngier, Z. An analysis of intensive forms in Hausa verbs. 'RO', 1965, 29 (2), 31-51.

42 Galadanci, M.K. 'An Introduction to Hausa Grammar'. Lagos, 1976.

43 Galadanci, M.K. Ideophones in Hausa. 'HN', 1971, 1, 12-26.

44 Galadanci, M.K. The Structure and syntactic function of compound nouns in Hausa. 'AnL', 1972, 14, 147-54.

45 Goerner, M., Salman, Y. and Armitage, P. 'Two Essays on Arabic Loanwords in Hausa'. Zaria, 1966.

46 Gorshkova, N.N. Formanty ukazatel'nosti v yazyke Hausa. 'Semitskie yazyki'. Vol. 3. Moscow, 1966, 61-5.

47 Gouffé, C. A propos de haoussa /'y/. 'Word, 1969, 25, 131-9.

48 Gouffé, C. A propos de la phrase relative et de la phrase nominale en berbère et en haoussa. 'GLECS', 1963-6, 10, 222-56.

49 Gouffé, C. Compléments et précisions concernant le haoussa dans le cadre de l'Essai comparatif de M. Marcel Cohen. 'GLECS', 1969-70, 14, 27-43.

50 Gouffé, C. Contacts de vocabulaire entre le haoussa et touareg. In Caquot, A. et al. (eds). 'Actes du premier Congrès Internat. de Linguistique Sémitique et Chamito-Sémitique', Paris, 16-19 Juillet 1969'. The Hague, 1974, 357-80.

51 Gouffé, C. Deux notes grammaticales sur le parler haoussa de Dogondoutchi (République du Niger). 'AÜ', 1968, 52 (1), 1-14.

52 Gouffé, C. La lexicographie du haoussa et le préalable phonologique. 'JAL', 1965, 4 (3), 191-210.

53 Gouffé, C. Les problèmes de l'aspect en haoussa. I. Introduction. Le problème de l'aoriste et de l'accompli. 'GLECS', 1963-6, 10, 151-65; II. Le problème de l'inaccompli I et II. 'GLECS', 1966-7, 11, 29-67; III. L'inaccompli négatif et l'ingressif. 'GLECS', 1967-9, 12-13, 27-51.

54 Gouffé, C. 'Manger' et 'boire' en haoussa. 'Revue de l'Ecole Nat. des lang. orientales', 1966, 3, 77-111.

55 Gouffé, C. Noms d'objects 'ronds' en haoussa. 'GLECS', 1963-6, 10, 104-13.

56 Gouffé, C. Observations sur le degré causatif dans un parler Haoussa du Niger. 'JAL', 1962, 1, 182-200.

57 Gouffé, C. Observations sur les emprunts au français dans les parlers haoussa du Niger. 'Actes du 8-e Congrès Internationale de Linguistique Africaine'. Vol. 2. Abidjan, 1971, 443-81.

58 Gouffé, C. Redoublement et réduplication en Haoussa: formes et fonctions. 'Bull. de la Soc. de Ling. de Paris', 1975, 70 (1), 291-319.

59 Gouffé, C. Remarques sur le syntagme démonstratif en haoussa. 'ASK', 170-9.

60 Gouffé, C. Sur les emplois grammaticalisés du verbe 'dire' en haoussa. 'GLECS', 1970-1, 15, 77-90.

61 Greenberg, J.H. Arabic loan-words in Hausa. 'Word', 1947, 3 (1), 85-97.

62 Greenberg, J.H. Linguistic evidence for the influence of the Kanuri on the Hausa. 'Journal of African History'. London, 1960, 1-2, 205-12.

63 Greenberg, J.H. Some problems in Hausa phonology. 'Lang.', 1941, 17 (4), 316-323.

64 Greenberg, J.H. 'Studies in African Linguistic Classification'. New Haven, 1955.

65 Greenberg, J.H. 'The Languages of Africa'. The Hague, 1966.

66 Gregersen, E.A. Some competing analysis in Hausa. 'JAL', 1967, 6 (4), 42-57.

67 Gregersen, E.A. 'Successes and Failures in the Modernization of Hausa Spelling. Advances in the Creation and Revision of Writing Systems'. The Hague - Paris, 1977, 421-40.

68 Gregersen, E.A. The palatal consonants in Hausa: internal reconstruction and historical inference. 'JAL', 1967, 6 (2), 170-84.

69 Gregersen, E.A. and Muhammed, A.L. The structural status of Hausa R sounds. 'HS', 415-20.

70 Günther, W. Reflections on sound-law and statistics, applied to the phenomenon of palatalisation in Hausa. 'Africana Marburgensia', 1978, 11 (2), 61-9.

71 'Hausa-russkii slovar'. Pod red. D.A. Ol'derogge. S prilozheniem kratkogo ocherka grammatiki yazyka Hausa, sost. I.A. Osnitskoi. Moscow, 1963.

72 Heine, B. 'Status and Use of African Lingua Francas'. Munich, 1970.

73 Herms, I. Zur Entwicklung des politischen Wortschatzes im Hausa. 'Linguistische Studien', 144-63.

74 Hill, C.A. Spatial perception and linguistic encoding. A case study in Hausa and English. 'SAfrL', 1974, Suppl. 5, 135-48.

75 Hiskett, M. The historical background to the naturalisation of Arabic Loan-words in Hausa. 'ALS', 1965, 6, 18-26.

76 Hodge, C.T. 'An Outline of Hausa Grammar'. Baltimore, 1947.

77 Hodge, C.T. Hausa-Egyptian establishment. 'AnL', 1966, 8 (1), 40-57.

78 Hodge, C.T. Hausa naa 'to be' or not 'to be'. 'African Review', Sierra Leone, 1969, 8, 152-62.

79 Hodge, C.T. Morpheme alternants and the noun phrase in Hausa. 'Lang.', 1945, 21 (2), 87-92.

80 Hodge, C.T. and Umaru, I. 'Hausa Basic Course', Washington, 1963.

81 Hoffman, C. Provisional check list of Chadic languages. 'Chadic Newsletter. Special issue'. Chadic working group, 1971.

82 Hofmann, I. Das Verhältnis der Langvokale zu den Kurzvokalen im Hausa. 'AÜ', 1965, 48 (3), 202-11.

83 Howeidy, A. 'Concise Hausa Grammar'. London, 1953.

84 Hugot, P. 'Cours élémentaire de Hausa'. Paris, 1957 (1st edn, 1953).

85 Hutchinson, J.P. Syntactic similarities across language families: a case from Hausa and Kanuri. 'HN', 1975, 5, 55-71.

86 Iordanidi, Y.G. K voprosu o vydelenii imeni sushchestvitel'nogo v yazyke Hausa. 'PF', 102-37.

87 Iordanidi, Y.G. Mestoimeniya v yazyke Hausa. 'V nauchnom poiske'. 'Uchenye zapiski'. Izd. Mosk. Gos. Instituta mezhdunarodnykh otnoshenii. Moscow, 1967, 560-74.

88 Jaggar, Ph. And what about ...? Topicalisation in Hausa. 'SAfrL', 1978, 9 (1) 69-81.

89 Jaggar, Ph. The nature and function of auxiliary verbs in Hausa. 'PChL', 557-87.

90 Jaggar, Ph. Thematic emphasis in Hausa. 'HN', 1976, 6, 63-74.

91 Jungraithmayr, H. Hausa, Ron, Angas: a comparative analysis of the aspect systems. 'AÜ', 1968, 52, 15-22.

92 Jungraithmayr, H. On root augmentation in Hausa. 'JAL', 1970, 9 (2), 83-8.

93 Jungraithmayr, H. and Möhlig, W.J.G. 'Einführung in die Hausa-Sprache. Unter Mitwirkung von A. Yusuf Katsina und A. Gwadabe'. Berlin, 1976.

94 Kirk-Greene, A.H.M. Neologisms in Hausa: a sociological approach. 'Africa', 1963, 33 (1), 25-44.

95 Kirk-Greene, A.H.M. The Hausa language board. 'AÜ', 1964, 47 (3-4), 187-203.

96 Kiselev, G.S. Nekotorye problemy etnogeneza Hausa. 'SE', 1977, 3, 22-31.

97 Klingenheben, A. Ablaut in afrikanischen Sprachen. 'ZES', 1930, 21, 81-98.

98 Klingenheben, A. Die Silbenauslautgesetze des Hausa. 'ZES', 1928, 18 (4), 272-91.

99 Klingenheben, A. Die Tempora Westafrikas und die semitischen Tempora. 'ZES', 1928-9, 19 (4), 241-68.

100 Korshunova, G.P. O slove iri v yazyke Hausa. 'VAF', 119-23.

101 Korshunova, G.P. and Uspenskii, B.A. K tipologii chastei rechi v Hausa: problema prilagatel'nogo. 'Yazyki Afriki'. Moscow, 1966, 264-87.

102 Kraft, C.H. 'A Study of Hausa Syntax'. Vols I-III. Hartford, Connecticut, 1963.

103 Kraft, C.H. An ethnolinguistic study of Hausa epithets. 'SAfrL', 1976, Suppl. 6, 135-46.

104 Kraft, C.H. Hausa sai and da - a couple of overworked particles. 'JAL', 1970, 9 (2), 182-204.

105 Kraft, C.H. The morpheme nà in relation to a broader classification of Hausa verbals. 'JAL', 1964, 3 (3), 231-40.

106 Kraft, C.H. Tone in Hausa. 'African Studies' (Johannesburg), 1970, 29, 129-38.

107 Kraft, C.H. Abubakar, S. 'An Introduction to Spoken Hausa'. Michigan State University, African Studies Center. African Language Monograph 5, 1965.

108 Kraft, C.H. and Kirk-Greene, A.H.M. 'Hausa' (Teach Yourself Books). London, 1973.

109 Kraft, C.H. and Kraft, M.G. 'Introductory Hausa'. Berkeley, University of California Press, 1973.

110 Landeroin, M. and Tilho, J. 'Grammaire et contes haoussas'. Paris, 1909.

111 Laptuchin, V.V. Einige Bemerkungen zur Entwicklung der Lexik im gegenwärtigen Hausa. 'Linguistic Studien', 164-76.

112 Laptukhin, V.V. O nekotorykh razlichiyakh v sovremennoi leksike dialektov yazyka Hausa Nigerii i Nigera. 'AF', 117-26.

113 Laptukhin, V.V. (sost.) 'Russko-Hausa slovar'. Pod red. Ado Gwadabe Kano. S prilozheniem ocherka 'Osnovnye morfologicheskie so-otvetstviya russkogo i Hausa yazykov', sost. Y.G. Iordanidi. Moscow, 1967.

114 Leben, W.R. A note on the base form of the Hausa verb. 'SAfrL', 1975, 6, 239-48.

115 Leben, W.R. Length and syllable structure in Hausa. 'SAfrL', 1977, 8, Suppl. 7, 137-43.

116 Leben, W.R. Parsing Hausa plurals. 'PChL', 89-105.

117 Leben, W.R. Suprasegmental and segmental representation of tone. 'SAfrL', 1971, Suppl. 2, 183-200.

118 Leben, W.R. The morphophonemic of tone in Hausa. Papers in African linguistics. Current Inquiry into Language and Linguistics I; Edmonton, Alb. and Champaign, Ill.; Linguistic Research, 1971, 201-18.

119 Lemeshko, B.G. Ob otritsanii v yazyke Hausa. 'AES', 1971, 8, 213-29.

120 Lemeshko, B.G. Spryazhenie glagola v yazyke Hausa. 'AES', 1966, 6, 226-50.

121 Lemeshko, B.G. Stativ v yazyke Hausa. 'AES', 1969, 7, 192-8.

122 Le Roux, J.M. 'Essai de dictionnaire français-haoussa et haoussa-français'. Algiers, 1886.

123 Lippert, J. Über die Stellung der Haussasprache unter den afrikanischen Sprachgruppen. 'Mitteilungen des Seminars für Orientalische Sprachen' (Berlin), 1906, 9, 334-44.

124 Lukas, J. Der II. Stamm des Verbums in Hausa. 'AÜ', 1964, 47 (3-4), 162-86.

125 Lukas, J. Über die Verwendung der Partikel sai im Haussa. 'AS', 108-17.

126 Marian, J. Les emprunts anglais dans le langue haoussa. 'Studia et acta orientalia, V-VI'. (Société des sciences historiques et philologiques de Roumanie.), 287-95.

127 Marré, E. 'Die Sprache der Hausa'. Vienna, 1901.

128 Maśka, Z. Versuch einer formalen Darstellung der Worttypen mit vollständiger Wurzelreduplikation im Hausa. 'FO', 1966, 8, 119-23.

129 Maxwell, J.L. 'Yau da gobe, A Hausa Grammar for Beginners'. Lagos, 1956.

130 McConvell, P. Relativisation and the ordering of cross-reference rules in Hausa. 'ASfrL', 1977, 8 (1), 1-31.

131 Meinhof, C. 'Die Sprachen der Hamiten'. Hamburg, 1912 (58-87).

132 Meyer-Bahlburg, H. Quantitative Untersuchungen zum I, II und IV Verbalstamm im Hausa. 'AÜ', 1973, 57 (2), 93-101.

133 Meyer-Bahlburg, H. Zur Stellung des Hausa innerhalb der afrikanischen Sprachen. Geschichte und ausgewählte Bibliographie. 'AÜ', 1975, 59 (1), 1-30.

134 Meyers, L.F. Aspects of Hausa tone. 'WPPh', 1976, 32.

135 Meyers, L.F. The Hausa particle 'ko'. An uncertainty modality. 'SAfrL', 1974, 5 (3), 247-64.

136 Meyrs, L.F. The particles sai and har; 'only', 'even' and 'until' in Hausa. 'ACAfrL', 213-21.

137 Meyrs, L.F. Tone patterns in Hausa: a re-analysis of Hausa downdrift. 'WPPh', 1974, 27, 47-62.

138 Migeod, F.W. 'A Grammar of the Hausa Language'. London, 1914.

139 Mischlich, A. 'Lehrbuch der Hausanischen Sprache (Hausa-Sprache)'. Berlin, 1902.

140 Mischlich, A. 'Wörterbuch der Hausasprache'. Vol. I: Hausa-Deutsch. Berlin, 1906.

141 Monsen, R.B. Semantic preliminaries to lexicography: a study of the Hausa verb. PhD diss., Columbia University, 1972.

142 Muhammad, D. A Vocabulary of literary terms in Hausa. 'HN', 1973, 3, 1-11.

143 Newman, P. Chadic extensions and predative verb forms in Hausa. 'SAfrL', 1977, 8 (3), 275-99.

144 Newman, P. Explaining Hausa feminines. 'SAfrL', 1979, 10 (2), 197-226.

145 Newman, P. Grades, vowel-tone classes and extensions in the Hausa verbal system. 'SAfrL', 1973, 4 (3), 297-346.

146 Newman, P. Hausa and Chadic. A reply. 'AIS', 1971, 12, 169-72.

147 Newman, P. Historical sound laws in Hausa and in Dera (Kanakuru). 'JWAL', 1970, 7 (1), 39-51.

148 Newman, P. Ideophones from a syntactic point of view/ Hausa and Tera/. 'JWAL', 1968, 5 (2), 107-17.

149 Newman, P. The Hausa negative markers. 'SAfrL', 1971, 2 (3), 183-95.

150 Newman, P. The historical development of medial /ee/ and

/oo/ in Hausa. 'Journal of African Languages and Linguistics' (Dordrecht), 1979, 1 (2), 173-88.

151 Newman, P. The non-correlation of tone and vowel height in Hausa. 'SAfrL', 1975, 6 (2), 207-13.

152 Newman, P. The two R's in Hausa. 'ALS', 1980, 7, 77-88.

153 Newman, P. Transitivity and intransitivity in Chadic languages. 'ASK', 188-200.

154 Newman, P., MA, R. Comparative Chadic: phonology and lexicon. 'JAL', 1966, 5 (3), 218-51.

155 Newman, P. and Newman, R.M. (comp.) 'Modern Hausa-English Dictionary'. Ibadan, Zaria, 1977.

156 Newman, P. and Schuh, R.G. The Hausa aspect system. 'Afroasiatic Linguistics' (Los Angeles), 1974, 1 (1).

157 Newman, R.M. Dictionaries of the Hausa Language. 'HN', 1974, 4, 1-25.

158 Newman, R.M. The two relative continuous markers in Hausa. 'SAfrL', 1976, Suppl. 6, 177-90.

159 Nuttall, C.E. 'Phonological Interference of Hausa with English'. Zaria, 1965.

160 Ogilvie, H.L. 'Helps to the Study of Hausa'. Jos, 1946.

161 Ol'derogge, D.A. Khamitskaya problema v afrikanistike. 'SE', 1949, 3, 156-70.

162 Ol'derogge, D.A. Proiskhozhdenie narodov tsentral'nogo Sudana (iz drevneishei istorii yazykov gruppy Hausa-kotoko). 'SE', 1952, 2, 23-38.

163 Ol'derogge, D.A. 'Proiskhozhdenie yazyka Hausa'. (Doklady sovetskoi delegatsii na V Mezhdunarodnom Kongresse antropologov i etnografov.) Moscow, 1956.

164 Ol'derogge, D.A. 'Yazyk Hausa. Kratkii ocherk grammatiki, khrestomatiya i slovar''. Leningrad, 1954.

165 Ol'derogge, D.A. 'Zapadny Sudan'. V. XV-XIX. Leningrad, 1960.

166 Osaji, D. Language imposition: sociolinguistic case study of the Hausa language in Nigeria. 'African Languages' (London), 1977, 3, 117-29.

167 Osnitskaya, I.A. K voprosu o formakh mnozhestvennogo chisla imeni sushchestvitel'nogo v yazyke Hausa. 'Voprosy filologii i istorii stran sovetskogo i zarubezhnogo Vostoka'. Moscow, 1961, 73-7.

168 Osnitskaya, I.A. Imennoe slovoobrazovanie v yazyke Hausa. 'AES', 1962, 4, 198-250.

169 Osnitskaya, I.A. Inversiya adresata deistviya v prostom i slozhnom predlozhenii yazyka Hausa. 'AES', 1966, 6, 279-84.

170 Paden, J.H. Language problems of national integration in Nigeria: the special position of Hausa. 'LProbl', 199-213.

171 Parsons, F.W. Abstract nouns of sensory quality and their derivatives in Hausa. 'AS', 373-404.

172 Parsons, F.W. An introduction to gender in Hausa. 'ALS', 1960, I, 117-36.

173 Parsons, F.W. Further observations on the 'causative' grade of the verb in Hausa. 'JAL', 1962, 1 (3), 253-72.

174 Parsons, F.W. Hausa and Chadic. 'HS', 421-58.

175 Parsons, F.W. Is Hausa really a Chadic language? Some problems of comparative phonology. 'ALS', 1970, 11, 272-88.

176 Parsons, F.W. Suppletion and neutralization in the verbal system of Hausa (the causative, the dative, and irregular verbs). 'AÜ', 1971/2, 55 (1/2), 49-97, 188-208.

177 Parsons, F.W. The operation of gender in Hausa: stabilizer, dependent nominals and qualifiers. 'ALS', 1963, 4, 166-207.

178 Parsons, F.W. The operation of gender in Hausa: the personal pronouns and genitive copula. 'ALS', 1961, 2, 100-24.

179 Parsons, F.W. The verbal system in Hausa. 'AÜ', 1960, 4 (1), 1-36.

180 Parsons, F.W. Towards a transformational grammar of Hausa. apers presented to the 5th West African Linguistic Congress. Accra, 1965, 1-56.

181 Pawlak, N. The semantic problems of 'intensive' forms in Hausa verbs. 'Africana Bulletin' (Warsaw), 1975, 23, 139-49.

182 Pike, K.L. 'Tagmemic and Matrix Linguistics applied to Selected African Languages'. Norman, 1970.

183 Pilaszewicz, S. 'Jezyk hausa'. Warsaw, 1971.

184 Pilszczikowa, N. Contribution à l'étude des rapports entre le haoussa et les autres langues du groupe nigéro-tschadien. 'RO', 1958, 22 (20, 75-99.

185 Pil'shchikova, N. 'Glagol'naya sistema yazyka Hausa'. Warsaw, 1957.

186 Pilszczikowa, N. La haoussa et le chamito-sémitique à la lumière de l'Essai comparatif de Marcel Cohen. 'RO', 1960, 24 (1), 97-130.

187 Pilszczikowa, N. Les verbes auxiliaires en haoussa. 'RO', 1960, 23 (2), 101-18.

188 Pilszczikowa, N. On the role of tonal contrast in the Hausa verb. 'JAL', 1972, 11 (2), 1-6.

189 Pilszczikowa, N. 'The Changing Form (grade 2) of the Verb in Hausa'. Warsaw, 1969.

190 Pilszczikowa-Chodak, N. On the correlation of tone and vowel height in Hausa: a reply to Newman. 'SAfrL', 1975, 6 (3), 315-21.

191 Pilszczikowa-Chodak, N. Tone-vowel height correlation and tone assignment in the patterns of the verb and noun plurals in Hausa. 'SAfrL', 1972, 3 (3), 399-421.

192 Porkhomovskii, V.Y. Nekotorye osobennosti foneticheskoi struktury slova v yazyke Hausa. 'VAF', 92-8.

193 Porkhomovskii, V.Y. Yazykovaya situatsiya v Severnoi Nigerii. 'Yazykovaya situatsiya v stranakh Afriki'. Moscow, 1975, 155-78.

194 Pugach, Z.L. Istoriya izucheniya yazyka Hausa. 'AES', 1963, 5, 200-22.

195 Rat, J.N. 'The Elements of the Hausa Language, or a Short Introductory Grammar in that Language'. London. 1889.

196 Robinson, C.H. 'Dictionary of Hausa Language'. I. Hausa-English, II. English-Hausa. Cambridge, 1899-1900 (the latest edn - 1969, reprint of 1925 edn).

197 Robinson, C.H. 'Grammar of the Hausa Language'. London, 1897.

198 Salim, B.A. Phonemic vowel neutralization in Hausa. 'PChL', 131-41.

199 Schachter, P. A generative account of Hausa ne/ce. 'JAL', 1966, 5 (1), 34-53.

200 Schön, J.F. 'Grammar of the Hausa Language'. London, 1862.

201 Schön, J.F. 'Vocabulary of the Hausa Language', London, 1853.

202 Schubert, K. Zur Bedeutung und Anwendung der Verbalparadigmen im Hausa und Kanuri. 'AÜ', 1971, 55 (3), 208-27.

203 Schuh, R.G. Rule inversion in Chadic. 'SAfrL', 1972, 3 (3), 379-97.

204 Schuh, R.G. Sound change as rule simplification? A study of consonant weakening in Kanakuru and in Hausa. 'ACAfrL', 95-101.

205 Schuh, R.G. The history of Hausa nasals. 'SAfrL', 1976, Suppl. 6, 221-32.

206 Shcheglov, Y.K. Logicheskie subyekt i predikat i sposoby ikh vydeleniya v yazyke Hausa. 'AF', 103-17.

207 Shcheglov, Y.K. 'Ocherk grammatiki yazyka Hausa'. Moscow, 1970.

208 Seidel, A. 'Die Haussasprache (Grammar and Vocabularies in German, English, and French)'. Heidelberg, 1906.

209 Silverstein, R.O. A strategy for utterance production in Hausa. 'SAfrL', 1976, Suppl. 6, 233-41.

210 Skinner, N. 'Hausa-English Pocket Dictionary', Zaria, 1968.

211 Skinner, N. 'Hausa for Beginners'. London, 1958.

212 Skinner, N. Hausa wani/wata/waɗansu and its semantic features. 'ACAfrL', 251-7.

213 Skinner, N. Kàmaa: an example of free variation in Hausa? 'JAL', 1970, 9 (1), 38-50.

214 Skinner, N. 'Kamus na Turanci da Hausa'. Zaria, 1976.

215 Skinner, N. Sources of Hausa /h/ initial. 'AnL', 1976, 18 (1), 1-7.

216 Skinner, N. The Hausa genitive morpheme as an exponent of gender: a query. 'HS', 389-98.

217 Skinner, N. The Hausa particle àmmā: an etymological note. 'JAL', 1967, 6 (2), 146-52.

218 Skinner, N. /ts/ and /k/ in Hausa. 'AnL', 1971, 13 (6), 301-10.

219 Smirnova, M.A. K voprosu o perekhodnosti v yazyke Hausa. 'AES', 1969, 7, 186-91.

220 Smirnova, M.A. Tonogrammy glagolov v Hausa-Angliiskom slovare Bargery. 'AES', 1971, 8, 236-40.

221 Stopa, R. Bushman substratum or Bushman origin in Hausa. 'FO', 1968, 9, 151-234.

222 Taylor, F.W. 'A Practical Hausa Grammar'. Oxford, 1959.

223 Umaru, A. and Bello, D. 'An Introduction to Classical Hausa and the Major Dialects'. Zaria, 1970.

224 Vishnevskaya, L.Y. Intonatsiya povestvovatel'nogo predlozheniya i intonatsionnogo voprosa v yazyke Hausa. 'ZPhon', 1968, 21, 567-8.

225 Vishnevskaya, L.Y. K voprosu o tonal'nosti yazyka Hausa. 'VAF', 77-91.

226 Vishnevskaya, L.Y. Morfologicheskii kauzativ v yazyke Hausa. 'Osnovnye problemy afrikanistiki. Etnografiya, Istoriya, Filologiya'. Moscow, 1973, 385-8.

227 Vishnevskaya, L.Y. Ob opyte eksperimental'nogo issledovaniya tonal'noi struktury predlozhenii yazyka Hausa. 'PF', 84-101.

228 Voznesenskaya, Y.A. K voprosu o yazykovykh kontaktakh Hausa i Fula v Nigerii. (Na materiale leksiki.) 'Vestnik Moskovskogo Un-ta. Vostokovedenie'. Moscow, 1975, 1, 65-73.

229 Voznesenskaya, Y.A. Nekotorye aspekty Hausa-Ful'bskogo dvuyazychiya. 'Istoriya vostochnych kultur'. Moscow, 1976, 126-32.

230 Wängler, H.-H. Über die Funktion der Tone im Hausa. 'ZPhon', 1963, 16, 231-40.

231 Wängler, H.-H. Zur Tonologie des Hausa. 'Schriften zur Phonetik, Sprachwissenschaft und Kommunikationsforschung', 1963, 6.

232 Westermann, D. 'Die Sprache der Haussa in Zentralafrika'. Berlin, 1911.

233 Weydling, G. 'Einführung ins Hausa'. Leipzig, 1942.

234 Yushmanov, N.V. 'Kratkaya grammatika yazyka Hausa'. Leningrad, 1935 (MSO.

235 Yushmanov, N.V. 'Stroi yazyka Hausa'. Leningrad, 1937.

236 Zhurkovskii, B.V. Reduplikatsiya i ideofony v yazyke Hausa. 'Sistema i urovni yazyka'. Moscow, 1969, 107-16.

237 Zhurkovskii, B.V. Tipologiya ideofona v Hausa. 'Fonologiya i morfonologiya afrikanskikh yazykov'. Moscow, 1972, 157-95.

238 Zima, P. A contribution to the analysis of verbal forms in a WNW Hausa dialect. 'AO', 1969, 37 (2), 199-213.

239 Zima, P. 'Digraphia': the case of Hausa. 'Linguistics. An International Review' (The Hague), 1974, 124, 57-69.

240 Zima, P. Final vowel duration of grade 6 verbs in Hausa. A phonetic problem with grammatical implications. 'Asian and African Studies' (Bratislava), 1974, 10, 49-58.

241 Zima, P. Hausa in West Africa. Remarks on contemporary role and functions. 'LProbl', 365-77.

242 Zima, P. 'Haustina'. Prague, 1973.

243 Zima, P. On syntactic alternation of verbal forms in Hausa. 'Mitteilungen des Instituts für Orientforschung' (Berlin), 1967, 13 (2), 188-98.

244 Zima, P. 'Problems of categories and word classes in Hausa. The paradigm of case'. Prague, 1972.

245 Zima, P. Remarques sur le consonantisme d'un parler haoussa du Niger. (Les problèmes de 'palatalisation'). 'Phonetica Pragensia' (Prague), 1974, 4, 123-32.

246 Zima, P. Research in the territorial and social stratification of African languages (Hausa and Songhay). 'ZPhon', 1975, 28 (3/4), 311-23.

247 Zima, P. Some problems of word order and grammar in Hausa. 'ASK', 217-23.

248 Zima, P. Some remarks on loanwords in modern Hausa. 'AO', 1964, 32 (4), 522-8.

249 Zima, P. The role of linguistics in a literary campaign in Africa. (Mainly on Hausa.) 'AO', 1975, 43, 210-22.